HB501   Amin, Samir.
A591713   The law of value and historical
           materialism / Samir Amin ; translated
           by Brian Pearce. -- New York :
           Monthly Review Press, c1978.
              133 p. : ill. ; 21 cm.
              Translation of La loi de la valeur
           et le matérialisme historique.
              Includes bibliographical
           references.
              ISBN 0-85345-470-1

              1. Capitalism. 2. Marxian
           economics. 3. Value.
           4. Historical materialism. I. Title.

HB501.A591713   335.4/11
                               78-15210

PWOCW   B/NA A D4-471724 0629139B   03/28/79

THE LAW OF VALUE
AND HISTORICAL MATERIALISM

SAMIR AMIN

THE LAW OF VALUE
AND HISTORICAL MATERIALISM

Translated by Brian Pearce

Monthly Review Press
New York and London

Library of Congress Cataloging in Publication Data

Amin, Samir.
  The law of value and historical materialism.

  Translation of La loi de la valeur et le
matérialisme historique.
    1. Capitalism.   2. Marxian economics.   3. Value.
4. Historical materialism.   I. Title.
HB501.A591713   335.4'11   78-15210
ISBN 0-85345-470-1

Monthly Review Press
62 West 14th Street, New York, N.Y. 10011
47 Red Lion Street, London WC1R 4PF

Manufactured in the United States of America

10 9 8 7 6 5 4 3 2 1

CONTENTS

INTRODUCTION. THE PURPOSE OF THIS WORK
AND THE ORDER IN WHICH THE
ARGUMENTS ARE PRESENTED   1

1. THE FUNDAMENTAL STATUS OF THE LAW OF VALUE   9

2. POLITICAL ECONOMY AND HISTORICAL MATERIALISM:
ACCUMULATION AND CLASS STRUGGLE   19

3. INTEREST, MONEY, AND THE STATE   37

4. GROUND RENT   45

5. THE IMPERIALIST SYSTEM AND THE DEVELOPMENT
OF A WORLD-SCALE HIERARCHY IN THE PRICE
OF LABOR POWER   57

6. THE THEORY AND PRACTICE OF MINING RENT IN THE
PRESENT-DAY CAPITALIST SYSTEM   69

APPENDIX. ONCE MORE ON THE QUESTION
OF TRANSFORMATION   83

CONCLUSION. THE GENESIS AND DISTRIBUTION
OF COLLECTIVE SURPLUS VALUE
IN THE IMPERIALIST SYSTEM   107

NOTES   127

INTRODUCTION.
THE PURPOSE OF THIS WORK
AND THE ORDER IN WHICH
THE ARGUMENTS ARE PRESENTED

1. Marx's writings appear at first sight to be divisible into works dealing with economics (a series of preliminary studies leading up to *Capital*—including Volumes II, III, and IV [*Theories of Surplus Value*], published posthumously) and works dealing with politics (*The Communist Manifesto*, and then a series of pamphlets surveying, in particular, the political history of the class struggles in France). The language of the economic writings seems to be that of classical (Ricardian) political economy, revised and corrected. It would appear that Marx is setting forth a series of economic laws explaining the way that capitalism functions, treating these laws as objective (that is, as imposing themselves upon society like natural forces), and articulating all these laws around a single "backbone"—the law of value. The language of the political writings, on the other hand, seems to be different from this. Here it is no longer a direct question of economic laws, but of clashes between social classes organized around political aims which are expressed in terms into which ideologies enter.

This seeming juxtaposition of two apparently irreducible discourses has given rise to a certain way of expounding

1

Marxism which is not only generally found in elementary textbooks and popular pamphlets, but also permeates the predominant trends in Marxist writing. According to this type of exposition there is, on the one hand, a correct economic science—Marxist political economy—which is a critique and complement of Ricardian economic science (regarded as inadequate) and is the absolute adversary of the so-called economic science known as the neoclassical school, regarded as an ideological discourse lacking in any scientific value. On the other hand, there is supposed to be a science of societies—historical materialism—based upon the fundamental proposition that class struggle is the driving force of history. These two "chapters" of Marxism are regarded as complementary, with their unity resulting from that of the method which inspires them both, namely, the philosophy of dialeccal materialism. Marx's philosophical works (meaning, mainly, *The German Ideology*) were, indeed, written earlier than his works on economic and political themes. This way of seeing Marxism may well have originated in its presentation by Kautsky, followed by Lenin, on the basis of its three "sources" (British political economy, French socialism, and German philosophy).

2. My intention here is not to refute this conception and substitute another, but merely to examine how, under capitalism, economic laws and class struggle are interlinked.

The subtitle of *Capital*—"A Critique of Political Economy"—does not mean a critique of a "bad (Ricardian)" political economy, with a view to replacing it with a "good (Marxian)" one, but a critique of so-called economic science, an exposure of its true nature (as what the bourgeoisie has to say about its own practice) and so of its epistemological status, an exposure of its limitations, and an invitation to realize that this alleged science, claimed to be independent of historical materialism, cannot possess such independence. On this matter I share the view expressed by Benetti, Berthomieu, and Cartelier.[1] As I see it, political economy is the outward form assumed by historical materialism (the class struggle) under capitalism. On the logical plane, historical materialism exists prior to economics, but class struggle under capitalism does not take place in a vacuum: it operates on an economic basis, and shapes laws which appear economic in character.

I shall study this articulation first as it is presented in *Capital* itself, that is, in the theory of the capitalist mode of production, and then in the reality of the capitalist system of our own day—in imperialism.

3. My thesis is: (a) that historical materialism constitutes the essence of Marxism, and therefore (b) that the epistemological status of the economic laws of capitalism is such that they are subordinate to the laws of historical materialism; (c) that under the capitalist mode of production economic laws possess a theoretical status different from that which they possess under precapitalist modes; and even (d) that, strictly speaking, economic laws are to be found only under the capitalist mode, so that "economic science" is not a general science of all modes of production but is the particular science of the capitalist mode;[2] (e) that the economic laws of capitalism do indeed exist objectively; and, finally (f), that these laws are governed, in the last analysis, by the law of value.

Thus, in my view, the class struggle under capitalism in general, and in the imperialist world system in particular, operates upon a definite economic basis and, in its turn, changes this basis. The absence here of any reference to dialectical materialism signifies, implicitly, that I reject the conception of philosophy known as "Diamat," deduced from the synthesized experience of "nature" and "society" and making possible the formulation of general laws common to both and, therefore, general laws of the human mind.

I regard dialectical materialism as a series of formulations which are deduced from the theory and practice of the class struggle under capitalism, and which therefore apply exclusively to society. The "materialism" of this conception is determined, in the last analysis, by the material basis, while the "dialectics" results from the interaction of opposites within the unity constituted by class struggle and economic laws. Under the capitalist mode, the material basis is manifested in its richest (meaning its most complex) form, that of economic laws, in contrast to the poor, simple, transparent form of the previous modes. We can deduce from this: (a) that historical materialism could be discovered only through the class struggles waged under capitalism; (b) that it enables us to understand the societies which preceded capitalism; but (c) that the dialectical mode of operation within the unity constituted by class struggles and material basis is manifested in precapitalist societies in a specific manner that differs from its manifestation under capitalism; and (d) that this mode of operation enables us to appreciate the nature of the aim that the proletariat must set itself to realize through the class struggle under capitalism, namely, the abolition of classes.

4. My argument consists of a principal thesis together with a subthesis which clarifies what this implies. The thesis maintains that, in the dialectical relations between historical materialism (class struggles) and the economic base, the two are not symmetrical: historical materialism is preeminent.

This thesis opposes two permanent tendencies which are at work among Marxists and which, in my view, constitute deviations from Marxism. The first of these is economism. According to this tendency, the economic system is completely determined by objective laws which operate with the force of natural laws. The class struggle, though admitted to exist, is seen as powerless to change these laws: it merely reveals their effects, and consequently functions as the "invisible hand" guiding the course of history. Here we have the philosophy that inspires social-democratic adaptation to "what is possible," and/or, complementing this, messianic expectation of a "catastrophic crisis" which is to bring about, with the force of necessity, the overthrow of capitalist relations.

Such a tendency engenders its own mechanical negation: subjectivist voluntarism. This tendency does away with the economic system altogether. Class struggle can accomplish anything whatsoever, depending entirely on political willpower. In contrast to economism, here it is ideology that determines the base. Class struggle, seen in this way, is governed by a sort of game theory.

My own thesis asserts that class struggle does not reveal the "necessary economic equilibrium," but determines one possible equilibrium among others. Class struggle, operating upon an economic base, in its turn shapes this base. There is no point in looking for the equilibrium corresponding to the economic optimum, since this concept itself lacks any scientific character. Furthermore, class struggle is not something superimposed upon the economy, as though the latter decides the nature and size of the cake, whereas the former defines the proportions in which the cake is doled out. In reality, the struggle over the sharing determines the nature, make-up, and form of the cake itself. Class struggle and economic laws together determine an equilibrium formed of contradictions which constitute its dynamic. In this analysis of dialectical interaction I shall show that the economic system is "closed" by accumulation, that is, dynamic equilibrium, thus introducing the modus operandi of demand.

The propositions here formulated in general terms will be

argued by means of illustrations relating to the principal domains of "economic equilibrium":

- Accumulation under the capitalist mode of production in its pure form (Chapter 2)
- Monetary equilibrium and the theory of the rate of interest (Chapter 3)
- Division of the surplus product between capitalists and landowners, and the theory of ground rent (Chapter 4)
- Accumulation on the world scale under the imperialist system and the emergency of a hierarchy of prices paid for labor power (Chapter 5)
- Division of the surplus product on the world scale between monopoly capital and the states of the periphery, and the theory of international mining rent (Chapter 6)

My thesis will thus be maintained on the terrain of the capitalist mode alone. It does not concern the dialectic of historical materialism and the economic base in general, nor that which applies to precapitalist societies, nor that which is peculiar to the transition to socialism. In a sense, therefore, it would be possible to complement the present study with two others:

(1) An analysis of the dialectical relation between class struggle and economic basis in precapitalist societies, and the problematic of relations between the development of the productive forces and the nature of production relations in precapitalist history (on this subject see "A quoi sert la réflexion sur les sociétés précapitalistes?").[3]

(2) An analysis of this dialectic in the transition to socialism on the world scale, and a discussion of the twofold contradictory nature of this transition in general and of the national liberation of the countries dominated by imperialism in particular (on this see "La bourgeoisie est-elle encore une classe montante?").[4]

As for capitalism in the strict sense of the word, the economic system can be described analytically either in empirical terms, on the basis of the economic categories presented in immediate reality (prices, profits, wages, supply and demand, and so on), or in terms seeking to relate these categories to the categories of value. Whichever procedure is followed, the economic system will appear as being determined, in the sense that it is not something indeterminant which results arbitrarily from class struggle but that class struggle operates on the basis of "economic laws."

This is where my subthesis comes in. I claim that the second type of analysis, carried out by Marx, which makes the law of value the backbone of the economic system, is not only possible (the value categories can be transformed into "immediate" ones) but superior. I shall show that value, and value alone, enables us to define and measure the development of the productive forces, relating this to necessary social labor, the objective common denominator. Only the law of value enables us to grasp the dynamic of the system: all analyses effected in terms which exclude it are doomed to a static, or metastatic, way of perceiving equilibrium.

So as not to overload my argument, I have relegated this subthesis to an appendix at the end of the book. It is implicit, however, in my first chapter.

1. THE FUNDAMENTAL STATUS OF THE LAW OF VALUE

1. What does the law of value state? That products, when they are commodities, possess value; that this value is measurable; that the yardstick for measuring it is the quantity of abstract labor socially necessary to produce them; and, finally, that this quantity is the sum of the quantities of labor, direct and indirect (transferred), which are used in the process of production. The concept of the commodity and the existence of the law of value, formulated in this way, are inseparably interconnected.

What does the law of value *not* state? That commodities are exchanged in proportion to their values; and that direct labor is present labor, whereas indirect labor is past labor crystallized in the means of production. (Volume II of *Capital* is based on the fact that the production of the means of production and the production of consumer goods are not successive in time, but simultaneous, this simultaneity defining the social division of labor in its most fundamental aspect.) This is why, when giving the solution to the problem of expanded reproduction, I have written that the surplus value generated in one phase should suffice to purchase the entire output of Department I during this phase "at the equilibrium price of the next phase."[1] What matters is not the value at which equipment has been produced in the past, but its social value, that is, its replacement value.

2. Possessing a certain value and being exchanged at that rate are two different notions. Marx says that, in the capitalist mode, commodities are exchanged in accordance with relations defined by their prices of production. Is this a contradiction? Does it mean making a pointless detour through value? My view is that neither is so.

Everyday experience shows us that a feather and a lump of lead dropped from the same height do not take the same length of time to reach the ground. Scientific physics teaches us that, as a result of the Earth's attraction, bodies in a vacuum all fall vertically, at the same speed. The falling of bodies as we observe it empirically is the result of a number of laws: the Earth's attraction, air resistance proportional to the surfaces of the bodies, and the direction and strength of the winds that determine the trajectory of a fall. These laws operate at different levels: the first operates at a level which is more fundamental than the others, but which is more difficult to ascertain, because it is less immediately obvious.

In the same way, prices of production result from a synthesis of the law of value, on the one hand, and the law of competition between capitals, on the other. The first-mentioned factor, the more fundamental of the two, would cause exchange to take place in accordance with values in a mode of production reduced to the sole reality of domination by the commodity, that is, simple commodity production. This mode does not exist in history, any more than a vacuum in nature is to be found on Earth. The capitalist mode, which cannot be reduced to this, is characterized by the presence, alongside domination by commodity, of fragmentation of capital and competition between capitals (and capitalists). Visible reality, in the form of prices of production, results from the combining of these two laws, which are situated on different levels.

Let us pursue this analogy. Concrete, actual prices result from the combination of the relations between prices of production and the specific conditions of competition, atomized or monopolistic, and all the attendant circumstances, whose role is like that of the winds in the falling of bodies.

We say that prices of production result from the combined action of two laws. Can this combination be expressed in a quantified transformation formula? In Volume III of *Capital* Marx does this, in his usual way, by giving numerical examples of various possible cases. He does not put forward successive approximations, but confines himself to a first approximation: constant capital stays measured in value, not in price. One can, without difficulty, solve the problem of transformation in an elegant way, without successive approximations, by means of a system of simultaneous equations. Is this operation legitimate? Certainly it is. Some people, though, think it is not, because in their view values and prices are not reducible to each other.[2] If this were so, the operation carried out by Marx would itself be illegitimate, and Volume III of *Capital* a blunder, a slip made by a non-Marxist Marx who had fallen victim to Ricardian economism. In reality, value is measurable, and the ratios between prices are homogeneous with ratios between values.

It cannot be said that value is a category of the process of production whereas price belongs to the process of circulation. Value and price are both categories of the process as a whole. Actually, value is realized, and consequently exists, only through exchange. It is in this overall process that concrete labor is transformed into abstract labor, and complex (compound) labor into simple labor. More generally, the view that value belongs only to the process of production is an "alibi" of Western-centered Marxism, which makes it possible to eliminate the problem of imperialism.

The only condition for transformation is that it should be possible to reduce concrete wage labor to a quantity of abstract labor. To say that this cannot be done is to condemn Marx, who does just this in Volume I of *Capital*, and to refuse to see that the actual tendency of capitalism is, indeed—by subjecting labor to the machine and downgrading labor skill on a mass scale—to reduce concrete forms of labor to abstract labor, as Harry Braverman has shown.[3]

It will be said that, simultaneously with the tendency mentioned, an opposite tendency is manifest: namely, the continuous creation of new forms of concrete labor, with an ever higher level of skill required in one part of labor (concerned with planning, organizing, research, and the like), the increasing reduction to wage-earner status of those workers situated between exploited labor and ruling capital, constant revision of wage differentials, and so on. It is certainly true that the "spread" of real wages cannot be explained by economic laws such as supply and demand, the cost of training, or unequal productivity, which are, as we shall see, merely so many ideological justifications.

The truth of the matter is that these phenomena, which run counter to the basic tendency, result from the class struggle, and especially from the initiatives taken by capital in this struggle: by organizing education on a basis of inequality it organizes scarcity, and on *this* basis it splits the ranks of the workers. The hegemony of capitalist ideology here fulfills the essential functions. It is not possible to understand the "economic laws" of capitalism without leaving the economic field and taking account of the total realm of historical materialism.

3. The question of transformation has been obscured by the fact that the writers who first tried to carry through the operation begun in Volume III of *Capital* also wanted to solve a problem which was easily shown to be insoluble:

transforming values into prices while retaining equality between the rate of profit and the rate of surplus value.[4]

If we abandon this requirement, we find no difficulty in transforming values into prices. Is the fact that the rate of profit necessarily differs from the rate of surplus value an embarrassing fact? On the contrary, it is normal for these two rates to differ: indeed, this result of transformation is one of the essential discoveries of Marxism.[5]

In the "transparent" modes of exploitation, the rate of exploitation is immediately obvious: the serf works for three days on his or her own land and for three days on the master's. Neither the serf nor the lord is blind to this fact. But the capitalist mode of exploitation is opaque. On the one hand, the proletarian sells labor power, but seems to be selling labor, and is paid for the eight hours of work put in, not just for the four that would be necessary for maintenance; on the other hand, the bourgeois realizes a profit which is calculated in relation to the capital owned, not to the labor exploited, so that this capital seems to the capitalist to be productive.

Sraffa's model appears to allow one to go still further. By replacing wages by their equivalent (the goods consumed by the wage earners), labor is made to disappear from the system of production equations: commodities are produced merely by means of commodities, without any intervention by labor (which remains subjacent), and the surplus is wholly attributable to capital, which has become the sole factor of production! Or else one can make the material inputs disappear by replacing them with their equivalent in past labor: what is then left is a system in which only a single factor appears, namely, labor—but this is dated, so that one is back with the factor of "productive time," as in Böhm-Bawerk.[6]

I have ascribed fundamental importance to this difference between the transparency of precapitalist exploitation and the opacity of the extortion of surplus labor under capital-

ism, and have based upon this distinction a series of propositions dealing respectively with (a) the different contents of
precapitalist ideology (alienation in nature) and capitalist
ideology (commodity alienation), and (b) the different relations between base and superstructure, with dominance by
the ideological instance in all the precapitalist modes and,
contrariwise, direct dominance by the economic base in the
capitalist mode. Thereby I have related the appearance of
"economic laws," and so of "economic science," to the
capitalist mode.[7]

Bourgeois economic science (neoclassical, i.e., vulgar,
economics) tries to grasp these laws directly, on the basis of
what is immediately obvious. It therefore takes capital for
what it seems to the capitalist to be, that is, a factor of
production, productive in itself, with labor as another factor
of production. This "science" does not stand up to the cri-
teria of formal logic. Wages are determined by the productivity of labor, and the productivity of labor is measured in
terms which imply these wages—a tautology, pure and
simple.[8] As for capital, it is not a homogeneous physical
magnitude, and the aggregation of different types of capital
has to be effected with reference to value, which presupposes
what is to be proved, namely, the existence and level of
profit—a second example of a circular argument.[9] The last
refuge is the claim that profit is the price of time, since
capital is anterior to production. Here, too, it has been shown
that capital produces value only if the rate of reward of time
is such as to permit this to happen. By overlooking the
social division of labor and replacing it with productions
succeeding each other in time, vulgar economics gets no-
where.[10]

4. But why, then, make this detour through value? Is it
done merely so as to understand the underlying nature of
capitalism, not just as an economic system but as an overall

social and political system? Could one not, if one's aim was merely to understand the economic laws of capitalism, apprehend directly the reality which is expressed in the price of production?

Serious bourgeois political economy, that of Ricardo, took this standpoint. Why not rest content with perfecting its presentation? Sraffa's model, defining directly the price of production of each product as the sum of the value of the inputs consumed, of the wages distributed, and of a profit proportionate to the capital advanced, and expressing the interdependence of all the relative prices—should not that be quite sufficient? And his conclusion, that real wages and the rate of profit are in inverse proportion to one another, when they are measured by a certain standard—is that not adequate?

One might confine oneself to replying that to understand capitalism means not only to understand its economic laws but also to understand the link between these laws and the general conditions of its social reproduction, that is, the way its ideological instance functions in relation to its base. The concept of value is a key concept, enabling one to grasp this reality in its full richness. Those who carry out the reduction which I here condemn always end up by conceiving socialism as nothing but "capitalism without capitalists."[11]

However, this argument, though sound, is not the only one available. At best Ricardo's model is capable of describing a static equilibrium: it cannot explain the system's dynamic. Indeed, the real wage and the rate of profit which it assumes are in inverse proportion to each other only under certain conditions, since the relation between them depends in its turn upon the yardstick chosen.

In Sraffa's model the productive system is given (the quantities of each commodity, $1, 2, \ldots i, \ldots n$, and the techniques used to produce them, including the inputs of direct labor), as is the real wage (the quantity of various goods that the hourly wage enables the wage earner to buy). Consequently, the relative prices and the rate of profit are determined in static equilibrium.

Actually, with a productive system reduced to two commodities (1) and (2), the unit prices of which are p_1 and p_2, wages (w) being replaced by the commodities constituting their counterpart, we have:

$$(a_{11}p_1 + a_{12}p_2)(l + r) = p_1$$
$$(a_{21}p_1 + a_{22}p_2)(l + r) = p_2$$

This system is perfectly determined. Its solution gives the relative price p_1/p_2 and the rate r.

However, depending on the standard adopted for measuring the product and the incomes of which it is composed, w and r stand in a relation to each other which is not necessarily decreasing and monotonic. That is the case only if one chooses one particular standard, namely, the net product. In that case, though, this standard which, for a given productive system, gives a linear relation (w, r), no longer gives this relation for the same system considered at a later stage of the development of the productive forces (when the coefficients a_{ij} alter). One cannot understand the dynamic which makes it possible to pass from one system to another.

To resort again to my analogy with physics: each Sraffian model describes a concrete situation in the same way as does a model formalizing the immediate results obtained from the observation of n bodies falling in an atmosphere. One cannot deduce any useful general law from the contemplation of a thousand Sraffian models—only the trivial conclusion that wages and profits are usually, but not always, in inverse proportion to each other.

This observation shows clearly that there is a certain continuity between Ricardian, classical, scientific economics and the degenerate neoclassical form. Marx was unable to "conserve" Ricardo while merely correcting him on a few points. He could do no more than to show the limitations of "economic science," so as to call for the problems being posed in a different way, in a different language, replacing the questions drawn from the economic field by other questions, drawn from another, broader field, that of historical materialism. This is the significance of *Capital*'s subtitle, "A Critique of Political Economy."

5. The economic problem cannot be reduced to the question of how relative prices are determined. Yet Ricardian analysis only allows one to answer *this* question: to say that, in a system which is in equilibrium, relative prices are determined by the distribution of income, this distribution being defined either by the real wage or by a rate of profit which is less than the maximum rate R, obtained when wages stand at zero.

The economic problem faces one with the need to answer other, much more important, questions than that. How does the development of the productive forces occur? Under the impact of what laws? What is its precise nature? How are we to measure its extent? And so on.

On this plane, the theory of value shows incontestable superiority. This theory alone enables us to make comparisons objectively, over time, between different productive systems, relating the magnitude of the product and of its components to the quantity of labor socially necessary, that is, to a standard which is independent of distribution.

Thus, whenever one wishes to analyze seriously the problem of accumulation—that is, of the progress of the productive forces, of the dynamic of capitalist growth, whether in its general aspect, the relation between the value of labor power and accumulation in the pure capitalist mode, or in one of its particular aspects (e.g., the relation between the level of rent and accumulation, or between the international distribution of value and accumulation on the world scale)— one is forced to argue in value terms. Every model of accumulation which is defined in empirical terms of prices, profits, etc., constitutes at best a submodel of partial equilibrium—useful, perhaps, for short-term analysis of bourgeois economic policy and the behavior of firms, but not enabling one to perceive the profound long-term tendencies of the effects of accumulation.

That is why, in the next chapter, I have kept to my model of accumulation in value terms, and adopted parameters describing the progress of the productive forces in terms of economy of social labor time. For the same reason, my analysis of the imperialist system of accumulation (Chapter 6) will be based upon arguments couched in value terms.

2. POLITICAL ECONOMY AND HISTORICAL MATERIALISM: ACCUMULATION AND CLASS STRUGGLE

1. After devoting Volume I of *Capital* to the foundations of the law of value, Marx concerns himself in Volume II with what might seem to be a purely "economic" argument. He tries, in fact, to show that accumulation can take place in a "pure" capitalist system, and to determine the technical conditions for dynamic equilibrium.

In Marx's illustrative examples, the system is characterized by a certain number of magnitudes and proportions, all of which belong strictly to the economic field. These magnitudes and proportions are: (a) the proportions in which labor power and means of production are distributed between the two departments which define the main basis of the social division of labor, making possible the simultaneous production of means of production and of consumer goods; (b) the proportions which characterize, for each department, the degree of intensity in the use of means of production by direct labor, which measures the level of development of the productive forces; (c) the evolution from one phase to another of these latter proportions, measuring the pace and direction of the progress of the productive forces; (d) the rate of exploitation of labor (the rate of surplus value).

Marx offers a series of examples in which the magnitudes are all given in value terms, and he is right to do so. But what he deduces from these examples—namely, the economic conditions for expanded reproduction—could, to some extent, be deduced in the same way from a model constructed directly in terms of prices of production, in which profit is shown in proportion to capital employed and not to labor exploited. Within this precise and limited context, the two arguments, both of them "economic," are equivalent to each other.

There is nothing, then, to prevent one from expressing directly—in terms either of value or of price—the general economic conditions for expanded reproduction, by formulating a system of linear equations in which the various variable magnitudes allocated to each department, defined correctly in relation to the parameters of sectoral distribution and of evolution from one phase to the next, are related to each other by the equality in value from one phase to the next in the respective supply of and demand for consumer goods and means of production.

2. I have done this[1] —in value terms, defining, by the Greek letters lambda (λ) and gamma (γ), two parameters for measuring the progress of the productive forces in each department and from one phase to the next, and then characterizing this progress by the increase in the physical quantity of use-values produced with a decreasing quantity of labor. The dynamic equilibrium is expressed by the twofold condition that the consumer goods produced during one phase must be absorbed by the demand during this phase (demand in physical quantities *and* in values), whereas the means of production produced during one phase must *exceed* in quantity the requirements for simple reproduction and be absorbed in the next phase—the incomes generated in one phase which are not allocated to consumption serving, in value

terms, to pay for the means of production which are to be installed for the next phase.

In the Appendix to "The End of the Debate" I therefore set out a model of expanded reproduction (with progress in the productive forces) which was defined simply, as follows:

Phase 1:

Department I: Production of means of production

$$1e + ab = pe$$

(meaning: a hours of direct labor, using 1 unit of equipment and raw material, produce p units of equipment).

Department II: Production of consumer goods

$$1e + bb = qc$$

(meaning: b hours of direct labor, using 1 unit of equipment and raw material, produce q units of consumer goods).

Phase 2:

The progress of the productive forces is defined by the capacity of the same quantity of direct labor (a and b) to set to work a larger mass of equipment and raw material and produce by this means a larger mass of equipment and consumer goods. Or, when λ and γ measure the progress of the productivity of labor (with λ and $\gamma > 1$):

$$1e + a\lambda b = pe$$
$$1e + b\gamma b = qc$$

Within this very general formal framework I established the following set of propositions:

1. A dynamic equilibrium is possible, provided only that labor power $(a + b)$ is distributed between the two departments in suitable proportions.

2. The pace of accumulation (measured by the growth in the production of equipment) conditions the level of employment (a conclusion opposite to that assumed by conventional economics).

3. Dynamic equilibrium presupposes that the consumer goods produced during one phase are purchased during that same phase (at the "prices"—values or prices of production—at which they were produced during the phase in question). The equipment goods produced during one phase are purchased at the beginning of the next, and accounted for at the prices of production of this second phase (devalorization of capital). Since the surplus value generated during one phase cannot be realized until the next phase, dynamic equilibrium requires centralized and correct management of credit.

4. If the entire economy is reduced to these two departments, dynamic equilibrium demands that there be an increase in wages, to be determined in a proportion that combines λ and γ. The rates of surplus value and the organic compositions evolve in line with λ and γ. The rate of profit is generally stable.

5. If real wages do not follow their necessary progression, equilibrium is possible only if a third department, for unproductive consumption of surplus value, develops parallel with Departments I and II.

From this general schema of expanded reproduction I have thus deduced a first conclusion, namely, that dynamic equilibrium requires the existence of a *credit system* which places at the capitalists' disposal the income that they will realize during the next phase.[2] This demonstration establishes the status of the Marxist theory of money and gives precise content to the Marxist (anti–quantity-theory) proposition that the supply of money adjusts itself to the demand for money (to social need), by linking this social need with the conditions for accumulation. How important this proposition is remains unperceived by those theorists who do not dare to *continue* Marx's work, but prefer to confine themselves to *expounding* it.[3] Moreover, this precise integration of credit into the theory of accumulation is the *only* answer to the "market question" raised by Rosa Luxemburg.[4]

Once this has been established, the generalized schema of expanded reproduction enables us to distinguish the economic conditions for dynamic equilibrium. These conditions can also be deduced from the illustrations given in Volume II of *Capital*. The mathematical model, though more elegant and more rapid, is no richer.

The demonstration presupposes a definite initial situation (phase I), namely: (a) given techniques of production, with known productivity, measured by the quantity of use-values produced by a quantity of social labor; (b) a social distribution of labor which is given by virtue of a certain quantitative distribution of the productive forces between the two departments; (c) a given rate of surplus value; (d) a determined level of real wages, resulting from the combination of (a) and (c); and (e) advances in the productivity of labor in each department, λ and γ, representing changes in techniques of production made between phase I and phase II. All these conditions, being defined in relation to value, are "objective."

It can then be seen that equilibrium of supply and demand when phase II is reached is possible only if the rate of surplus value (and therefore the real wage as well) is established at a definite level, a function of λ and γ and of the parameters representing the initial situation.

The schema of expanded reproduction thus seems to reveal that precise economic laws do exist which, like any other laws, have an objective existence, that is, impose themselves willy-nilly on everyone.

If we accept the framework of this argument, what will happen in the event that, for whatever reason, the rate of surplus value (and the real wage) is established at a level other than that "necessary" for equilibrium? If the real wage is too high, it will not be possible to achieve expanded reproduction during phase II: on the contrary, reproduction will be reduced, with the production of means of production shrinking from one phase to the next until social production grinds to a standstill. If the real wage is too low, production cannot be absorbed during the next phase: there is a crisis of overproduction, and investment ceases as a result of the fall in the rate of profit, anticipating difficulties in realization. The first of these cases serves as an argument to those who see political economy as a science of the organization of production which is equally valid for the running of a socialist society, and justifies their reduction of socialism to a capitalism without capitalists. The second case corresponds to Tugan-Baranovsky's absurd "merry-go-round."[5]

To conclude, the importance of Volume II of *Capital*, *as it stands*, is essential: it shows that, in the capitalist mode, social reproduction appears first and foremost as *economic* reproduction. Whereas in the precapitalist modes, in which exploitation was transparent, reproduction implied direct intervention from the level of the superstructure, that is not so here. This qualitative difference needs to be emphasized.

3. What happens if we substitute for this analysis, carried out within a framework strictly inspired by Volume II of *Capital*, an analysis conducted directly in price terms, using a model of the Sraffian type?

The difference between the two methods is situated on two

planes, which must be carefully distinguished: (a) the substitution of prices for values, and (b) the adoption of a system of production with n branches instead of the two departments specializing in the production, respectively, of equipment goods and of consumer goods.

A. SRAFFA'S SCHEMA

Let us assume that there are two lines of production, (1) and (2), each of which produces both producer goods and consumer goods, and that a_{ij} = the coefficients of inputs necessary for the production of these goods; p_1 and p_2 = their unit prices; w = the unit wage (the quantities of labor being assigned by the coefficients a_{01} and a_{02}), and r = the rate of profit. We then have:

$$(a_{11}p_1 + a_{12}p_2 + a_{01}w)(1 + r) = p_1$$
$$(a_{21}p_1 + a_{22}p_2 + a_{02}w)(1 + r) = p_2$$

To this system corresponds the following system of values:

$$a_{11}v_1 + a_{12}v_2 + a_{01} = v_1$$
$$a_{21}v_1 + a_{22}v_2 + a_{02} = v_2$$

Let it be remembered that since the two products (1) and (2) are not destined by nature, one for use as equipment and the other for consumption, this system does not describe an equilibrium of supply and demand for each department. The conditions for *that* equilibrium, which are assumed to be achieved, are external to the model.

We define two parameters of improvement in productivity, π_1 and π_2, specific to each of the branches (1) and (2). Let us assume, for simplicity, that it is the same, π, in both cases. Let us go on to assume that the system of values for phase I is as follows:

$$0.2v_1 + 0.4v_2 + 0.4 = v_1$$
$$0.5v_1 + 0.1v_2 + 0.6 = v_2$$

from which we get $v_1 = 1.15$ and $v_2 = 1.30$.

Assuming that the same quantity of direct labor becomes capable of setting to work twice as much equipment and raw material (and, for simplicity, in the same proportions aij), so as to provide twice the quantity of end products (that is, if $\pi = 0.5$), we have for phase II:

$$0.4v_1' + 0.8v_2' + 0.4 = 2v_1'$$
$$1.0v_1' + 0.2v_2' + 0.6 = 2v_2'$$

from which we get $v_1' = 1.07$ and $v_2' = 1.65$.

The table below will then show the evolution of the system of values obtained with the same global quantity of labor, left unchanged:

	Phase 1	*Phase 2*
Production	$1.0v_1 + 1.0v_2 = 2.45$	$2.0v_1' + 2.0v_2' = 5.44$
− Productive consumption	$0.7v_1 + 0.5v_2 = 1.45$	$1.4v_1' + 1.0v_2' = 3.14$
= Net product	$0.3v_1 + 0.5v_2 = 1.00$	$0.6v_1' + 1.0v_2' = 2.30$

The results, meaning the increase in the net product (from

1.00 to 2.30), are independent of distribution (no assumption having been made regarding wages or the rate of profit).

If, however, we examine the evolution of a system expressed in prices, we have to introduce an assumption regarding *the way income is distributed*.

The previous system, expressed in price terms, namely:

$$(0.2p_1 + 0.4p_2 + 0.4w)(1 + r) = p_1$$
$$(0.5p_1 + 0.1p_2 + 0.6w)(1 + r) = p_2$$

completed by an assumption regarding wages, e.g., that:

$$w = 0.2p_1 + 0.2p_2$$

can be reduced to a system of "production of commodities by means of commodities only" which here is as follows:

$$(0.28p_1 + 0.48p_2)(1 + r) = p_1$$
$$(0.62p_1 + 0.22p_2)(1 + r) = p_2$$

the solutions of which are $p_1/p_2 = 0.93$.

For the next phase the system becomes:

$$(0.4p_1' + 0.8p_2' + 0.4w')(1 + r') = 2p_1'$$
$$(1.0p_1' + 0.2p_2' + 0.6w')(1 + r') = 2p_2'$$

The results (relative prices and rate of profit) will depend on the way that wages evolve. If we assume an unchanged real wage, that is, if

$$w' = w = 0.2p_1' + 0.2p_2'$$

the reduced system becomes:

$$(0.24p_1' + 0.44p_2')(1 + r') = p_1'$$
$$(0.56p_1' + 0.16p_2')(1 + r') = p_2'$$

the solutions of which are $p_1'/p_2' = 0.98$, from which we get the comparative table, established in price terms, given below:

	Phase 1	*Phase 2*
Production	$1.0p_1 + 1.0p_2 = 2.08$	$2.0p_1' + 2.0p_2' + 4.04$
− Productive consumption	$0.7p_1 + 0.5p_2 = 1.24$	$1.4p_1' + 1.0p_2' = 2.42$
= Net product	$0.3p_1 + 0.5p_2 = 0.84$	$0.6p_1' + 1.0p_2' = 1.62$
of which, wages	$0.2p_1 + 0.2p_2 = 0.42$	$0.2p_1' + 0.2p_2' = 0.40$
and profits	$0.1p_1 + 0.3p_2 = 0.42$	$0.4p_1' + 0.8p_2' = 1.22$

It will be noted that comparison between the two phases is obscured by the fact that the solution of the system gives relative prices, p_1/p_2 and p_1'/p_2', which differ according to the evolution of wages. We do know, from our assumption, that the system of phase II will enable us to obtain, with the same total quantity of labor, twice as much physical product (use-values) from (1) and (2). But if we assume $p_1 = p_1' = 1$, we have $p_2 \neq p_2'$, since p_1/p_2 and p_1'/p_2' both depend on the way distribution takes place. Here $p_2 = 1.08$ and $p_2' = 1.02$.

The net product, measurement of the growth in value of which is independent of distribution (in my model, this net product increases in value terms from 1.00 to 2.30), here increases from 0.84 to 1.62 (a growth rate of 193 percent) when we analyze the evolution of the system in price terms, with the given assumption regarding wages.

It is because of these uncertainties in measurement of the development of the productive forces in price terms that I prefer models constructed in terms of value, the only certain standard.

B. A MARXIAN MODEL IN PRICE TERMS

The major defect of analysis in price terms compared with analysis in terms of value is not due to the "open" character of Sraffa's model (meaning that the dynamic equilibrium of supply and demand for each product—equipment goods and consumer goods—is not formulated as an internal condition of the model but simply assumed to be realized externally), in contrast to the "closed" (full-circle) character of Marx's model (in which the equilibrium in question is formalized in the model itself). This defect is due to the substitution of prices, which depend on distribution, for values, which do not so depend. Thereby, the concept of improvement in the productivity of labor (as the measure of development of the productive forces), which is perfectly objective in Marx's practice (it does not depend on the rate of surplus value) is no longer objective in Sraffa's model or in any other model constructed in price terms.

Furthermore, the Sraffian framework does not lend itself to analysis of the conditions for dynamic equilibrium, since unlike Marx's framework it is not concerned with the equilibrium of supply and demand for each type of product. It is therefore impossible to deduce from it the propositions set out above concerning expanded reproduction. What it offers is a meager, empirical model which serves, at best, to describe an evolution that has been observed, but not to infer from this any laws of evolution.

Let us go back to our "Marxian" model. The conditions of distribution (the rate of surplus value) have been introduced into it, not in order to define the progress of the productive forces from one phase to another, but in order to define the conditions for equilibrium between supply and demand. It would be possible, therefore, to retain Marx's framework—that is, argument in terms of Department I and Department II—while formulating the magnitudes as prices.

Actually, dynamic equilibrium of supply and demand for the products of Departments I and II implies that distribution be spelled out. It can be formulated in terms of wages and surplus values (the surplus values being proportionate to the labor power employed in each department), in which case the magnitudes (net product and the like) are measured in values; or it can be formulated in terms of wages and profits (the profits being proportionate to the capital held in each department) in which case the magnitudes are measured in prices.

This transformation retains the four sets of results relating to the conditions for dynamic equilibrium established on the basis of the model in value terms, namely: that equilibrium is possible, that it assumes an active role being played by credit, that it implies an increase in wages related to the increase in productivity, or, failing that, the development of an unproductive sector to absorb the surplus. It remains the case that the increase in productivity in question is no longer defined objectively.

Whether it be constructed in terms of value or of price, Marx's model is closed by simultaneously taking account of the distribution of income and of the structure of demand resulting from this. Contrary to a current misconception, Marx does not disregard demand (and therefore use-value): it is perfectly well integrated into his overall diagram.

4. There has been no question so far of the class struggle. This is, indeed, absent from the direct discourse of Volume II of *Capital*.

One attitude that can be taken in this connection is that the class struggle setting bourgeoisie and proletariat against each other over the division of the product (the rate of surplus value) is subordinate to economic laws. The class struggle can, at most, only reveal the rate of equilibrium that is objectively necessary. It occupies, in this context, a position comparable to that of the "invisible hand" of bourgeois economics. The language of the "universal harmony" of social interests is replaced by that of the "objective necessities of progress."

This attitude is obligatory for anyone who considers the premises of the argument set out above to be ultimate truths—that is, who accepts that production techniques and their progress constitute data external to the economic problem. This is the normal attitude of bourgeois economics. But this is also, of necessity, the view of those who see the development of the productive forces as an independent force (the expression of progress) which is either promoted or slowed down by given production relations (requiring, in the latter case, a transformation of these relations so as to let the development realize its full potential), without really accepting that the *type* of development of the productive forces (and not merely its *pace*) is determined by production relations.

What we have here is a reduction of Marxism to the so-called Marxist (or, rather, Marxian) political economy which is fashionable in the English speaking world under the name of "Marxian economics."[6] According to this view, there are economic laws which constitute objective necessities, irrespective of the class struggle.

On such a basis, however, it is no longer possible to conceive of a classless society in the true sense, since it appears as a society identical with class society. The progress of the productive forces continues to dominate it, just as this progress has been dominant throughout history. This progress has its own laws: an ever more intensified division of labor, in the forms we know well. Capitalism is seen as guilty only of not being able to carry forward the march of progress effectively enough. As for those writings of Marx in which he criticizes sharply the shortsightedness of the Pharisee who cannot imagine a future in which no one is exclusively an artist or a turner, they are so much utopian daydreaming. Capitalism is seen as, basically, a model for eternity, blameworthy only for the social "wastage" constituted by the capitalists' consumption, and for the anarchy caused by competition between capitals. Socialism will put an end to these two abuses by organizing, on the basis of state-centralized ownership of the means of production, a system of "rational planning."

How are we to arrive at this statist mode of production—the highest stage of evolution, a wise submission to "objective laws," for the greater good of society as a whole? By the road of reformism. On the one hand, absence of organization of the working class makes it easy for the capitalists to misuse their power by refusing to grant the wage increases which are objectively necessary for dynamic equilibrium. On the other hand, trade unions, by imposing a "social contract" governing the distribution of the gains of productivity, prepare the way for formal expropriation of the unnecessary capitalists, after having first served as a school of management for the cadres and elites who represent the proletariat and whose task it is to organize and command.

5. There is a second possible attitude. Reacting against this type of analysis, one proclaims the supremacy of the class struggle, moving it to the forefront of the stage. Wage levels, it is held, result not from the objective laws of expanded reproduction, but directly from the conflict between classes.

Accumulation adjusts itself, if it can, to the outcome of this struggle—and, if it can't, then the system suffers crisis, that's all.[7] This attitude is, at bottom, undoubtedly the correct one. It reminds us that the progress of the productive forces (its pace and the directions it takes) is not some independent exogenous factor, but one that results from class struggle and is embodied in production relations—that it is modulated by the ruling classes. This thesis reminds us that the Taylorism of yesterday and the automation and "technological revolution" of today are responses to working-class struggle, as are also the centralization of capital, imperialism, the relocation of industries, and so on.

However, although this attitude is basically correct, if it is dominated exclusively by concern with counterbalancing the first attitude, it runs the risk of falling in its turn into the error of one-sidedness. So long as capitalism has not been overthrown, the bourgeoisie has the last word in class struggles. This must never be forgotten. It means that unless crises lead to the overthrow of capitalism—which is always a *political* act—they must always be solved in the bourgeoisie's favor. Wages which are "too high" are eroded by inflation, until the working class, exhausted, gives in. Or else "national unity" makes it possible to shift the burden of the crisis onto others' backs.

These "realities" then make themselves felt as "objective laws." This is what the radicalized petty bourgeoisie tries to ignore when it remains satisfied with proclaiming that "the class struggle occupies the forefront of the stage," without troubling to define the nature and conditions of the struggles involved.

For a view of the matter which is not one-sided we need to appreciate that the class struggle proceeds, in the first place, from a given concrete situation, reflecting the reality of a particular economic basis; that this struggle then modifies the economic basis; but that, so long as the capitalist system still exists, this modification necessarily remains confined by the laws of economic reproduction of the system. An alteration in wages affects the rate of profit, dictates a type of reaction on the part of the bourgeoisie which is expressed in given rates of "progress" (λ and γ) in given directions, changes the social division of labor between the two departments, and so on. But so long as we remain within the setting of capitalism, all these modifications respect the general conditions for capitalist reproduction. In short, *the class struggle operates on an economic base and shapes the way this base is transformed within the framework of the immanent laws of the capitalist mode.*

The schemata of expanded reproduction illustrate this fundamental law that the value of labor power is not independent of the level of development of the productive forces. The value of labor power must rise as the productive forces develop. This is how I understand the "historical element" to which Marx refers when writing of how this value is determined. The only other logical answer to that question is the rigid determination of the value of labor power by "subsistence" (as in Ricardo, Malthus, and Lassalle).

But this objective necessity does not result spontaneously from the functioning of capitalism. On the contrary, it constantly comes up against the real tendency inherent in capitalism, which runs counter to it. The capitalists are always trying to increase the rate of surplus value, and this contradictory tendency is what triumphs in the end. This is how I understand what is meant by the "law of accumulation" and the "relative and absolute pauperization" by which it is manifested. Facts show the reality of this law—but on the scale of the world capitalist system, not on that of the imperialist centers considered in isolation: for whereas, at the center, real wages have risen gradually for the past century, parallel with the development of the productive forces, in the periphery the absolute pauperization of the producers exploited by capital has revealed itself in all its brutal reality. But it is there, precisely, that the pro-imperialist tendency among Marxists pulls up short, for it is from that point onward that Marxism becomes subversive. (This problem of the class struggle in relation to accumulation on the world scale will arise again in Chapter 5.) The consequences that follow from this contradiction constitute the real problems—which are of no interest to dogmatic professorial Marxism or, for that matter, to the revisionist and cryptorevisionist labor movement. The most fundamental of these consequences is the constitution of the world system on the basis of unequal development.

The second consequence is that capital overcomes this contradiction by developing a "third department," the function of which is to take in hand the excess surplus value which cannot be absorbed in Departments I and II, owing to the inadequate increase in the real wages of the productive workers. This decisive contribution by Baran and Sweezy has never been and can never be understood by any of those who decline to analyze the immanent contradiction of capitalism in dialectical terms.[8] They will reject this new fact because it is not to be found in *Capital*. But are they not, in doing this, rejecting also imperialism—which is not in *Capital* either?

3. INTEREST, MONEY, AND THE STATE

1. In Volume III of *Capital* we find that Marx's language undergoes a sudden change. It is no longer a question of commodity fetishism and alienation, or of the value of labor power and surplus value. Marx speaks to us now of social classes as they appear in concrete reality—of workers, industrial capitalists, commercial capitalists, moneylenders, landowners, peasants, and so on—just as he speaks to us of incomes as they can be perceived directly, through statistics—such as wages, the industrialist's and the merchant's profit, the rate of interest, ground rent, and so on. This change of tone reflects the transition from the theory of the capitalist mode to an initial analysis of the central capitalist forms.[1] It is also the moment when he begins to go beyond the political economy he is questioning and to develop his argument in terms of historical materialism.

I have examined this transition in its fundamental aspect: the "determination" of the rate of profit and of the value of labor power through the struggle between the fundamental classes, on the basis of the laws of accumulation and of the fragmentation of the control of capital (Volume II and the chapters of Volume III dealing with "transformation"). I shall now examine it in relation to the two other questions which are dealt with in Volume III: the rate of interest (Chapter 3) and ground rent (Chapter 4).

2. What Marx has to say about money and interest is scattered through various parts of his work. In the drafts for *Capital* (especially the *Grundrisse*) Marx gives us a series of reflections which are as concrete as can be: observations on the policy regarding discount rates followed by the Bank of England or the Banque de France at particular moments of history, critical thoughts relating to the commentaries of the principal economists of the time on these policies, and so on. No explicit theory is expounded. In Volume III, however, Marx puts before us a theory of the rate of interest which runs like this: (a) interest is the reward of money capital (not of productive capital); (b) it is therefore a category of distribution; (c) the rate of interest is determined by the interplay of supply and demand for money capital, in which two subclasses, lenders and borrowers, confront each other; (d) this rate is indeterminate and can be situated at any point between a floor (zero interest) and a ceiling (a rate of interest equal to the rate of profit).

This theory seems to me inadequate. Indeed, Marx does not show any particular fondness for resorting to "supply and demand," and when he does do so he usually raises at the outset the question: What real forces determine this supply and this demand? Here, however, we find nothing of the sort.

The theory is inadequate, in the first place, because the floor and the ceiling in question are too low and too high, respectively. The rate of interest cannot be zero because, if it were, there would be no lenders. It cannot be equal to the rate of profit, for then the productive capitalists would cease to produce, and so they would not borrow.

Above all, though, it is inadequate because the resort to postulating two subclasses of capitalists, imagined as being independent of each other, contradicts Marx's thesis on money. Marx considers the demand for money, the social need for a certain quantity of money, as being determined *a priori* by the conditions of expanded reproduction, with lines of production and prices determined independently of the quantities of money available. This rigorously anti-quantitativist position has been accepted by all Marxists: it has merely been continued and made more precise in relation to the schemata of expanded reproduction (see Chapter 2). It suggests, moreover, that the supply of money adjusts itself to this need, this demand. The creation and destruction of credit by the banking system fulfills this function.

If that is the case, one cannot see how the confrontation of supply and demand could in any way determine the rate of interest. We do not observe two independent subclasses meeting in a market for lending and borrowing. What we do observe is, on the one hand, those who demand—namely, the productive capitalists as a whole, their demand being dependent on the extent to which their own capital is insufficient—and, on the other hand, institutions which respond to their demand. When and what do these institutions represent? They do not represent a subclass, that of the bankers. Even if the banks are private establishments, and even if the bank of issue to which they are subject, since it is the ultimate lender, is also a private establishment, state policy has always intervened (even in the nineteenth century) to regulate this supply of money. The monetary system of capitalism has always been relatively centralized.[2] The point is that the bank, like the state, represents the collective interest of the bourgeois class. The "two hundred families" who held shares in the Banque de France were not merely moneylending capitalists; they also constituted, through this bank, the principal nucleus of the French bourgeoisie. Thus, we have here a contrast not between two subclasses but between the capitalists as individuals in rivalry with one another (the fragmentation of capital) and the capitalist class organized collectively. The state and the monetary institutions are not the expression of particular interests counterposed to other particular interests, but of the collective interests of the class, the means whereby confrontation between separate interests is regulated.

This regulation takes place in two domains where the collective interest of the class has precedence. The first is regulation of the trade cycle, and the second is regulation of international competition.

3. Regulation of the conjunction does not signify suppression of the cycle but, on the contrary, an ordered intensification of its scope, as a means whereby to maximize the pace of accumulation in time of prosperity and then to control this through liquidations, restructurings, and concentrations in time of crisis. This form of regulation is given ideological expression in the monetarist theories of the conjuncture—that is, in the attempt to rationalize the bourgeois practice of competition. The rate of interest appears as the supreme instrument for this regulation.

When, in a period of crisis, the state acts through the monetary system to impose an increase in the rate of interest, the central authority is intervening actively in economic life in the collective interest of capital. The raising of the rate of interest intensifies the crisis, multiplying bankruptcies. But it thereby accelerates the process of concentration of capital, the condition for the modernizing of the apparatus of production and the conversions which have become necessary. On the contrary, the reduction in the rate of interest in a period of prosperity accelerates the growth rate and enables the economy in question to derive maximum benefit from its restored external competitiveness.

4. The second domain is that of competition between national capitalisms. In the nineteenth century, in Marx's time, the rule of the game where international competition between the central capitalist formations was concerned was that of the gold standard (dual convertibility, internal and external). The flow this way and that of the yellow metal therefore responded to the difference between rates of interest. This flow constituted a source, positive or negative, of the supply of money at the disposal of the national monetary institutions. The practicing of monetary policies—that is, the manipulation of rates of interest—was therefore a means of intervening in the conduct of relations between the different national formations. Here, too, increasing the rate of interest in time of crisis helped to reestablish the external equilibrium when this was threatened during the conversion period, by attracting into the country "floating" capital from abroad.

Naturally, study of the domain of international competition cannot be reduced to abstract analysis of the mechanical relations linking different economic magnitudes, national and foreign: the volume and price of imports and exports, the flow of capital and its response to the rates of profit and of interest, and so on. In this domain it is always possible to claim that one can derive economic laws from empirical observation of the facts. Thousands of econometric models have been constructed with this end in view, but the results obtained from them have proved meager. In most cases, the laws inferred from observation of the past cannot be confirmed in the future and do not endow the public authorities with effective instruments of control. The reason for this is that what is essential often lies outside these models: the rate of progress of the productive forces, the results of the class struggle, and the effects of the latter upon the former.

It is my opinion that the reason why Marx did not construct an economic theory of international relations is to be sought here. As we know, Marx did say, in the *Grundrisse* and in several preliminary sketches for *Capital*, that there would be a chapter on international relations, but he never wrote such a chapter. Was this because he did not have the time? I think, rather, that he gave up his intention because he realized that no economic theory of world trade was possible. Before tackling the economic aspect of international relations (the "economic appearances," the visible part of the iceberg), it was necessary to carry out a thorough analysis in the terms of historical materialism. Just as an analysis of the class struggle on the scale of the national formations had provided the basis for the theory of the capitalist mode, so an analysis of the class struggle on the scale of the world capitalist system is prerequisite for an analysis of the world economy. But an "economic" theory of international relations is impossible.[3] After rejecting the economic theories of adjustment of the balance of payments, I myself decided in favor of a line of research directed at the class struggles on the world scale which shape the structural adjustments between national formations within the framework of which the apparent economic laws operate. I shall have occasion to come back to this problem when I examine the questions of historical materialism and their relation to the law of value operating on the scale of worldwide accumulation.

5. The two domains—the internal conjuncture and external competitive capacity—are closely linked. This is why the instrument of monetary policy is still the instrument *par excellence* of the economic policy of the bourgeois state.

Here, then, are two domains in which forces are at work that determine the rate of interest: two domains which belong to the realm of historical materialism, not of economics. Economic theory (meaning *pure* economic theory—

that is, a science independent of historical materialism) ignores the state, the collective expression of the bourgeoisie, and the national states of the central bourgeoisies which are in conflict with one another. But Marxism never fails to take into account these aspects of social reality, and never deals with them in isolation from an economy which is supposed to ignore them.[4]

Bourgeois economistic ideology has produced, in this domain, dozens of theories, thousands of models, and as many recipes and schools of thought. But the characteristic feature of all these theories, and the reason they remain ideological, is that they avoid the role played by crisis in the restoration of order (because one must not cast doubt on the harmonious character of capitalist growth: crisis has always to be presented as something accidental) and also the nature of the struggle over shares in domination of the world (because bourgeois ideology counterposes economics, where peaceful competition is supposed to reign, to politics, which is admitted to be the scene of evil aggressive behavior.)

Undoubtedly, too, the precise content of these theories has had to be adapted, more or less, to the actual evolution of the system. The changes in the predominant forms of competition (the formation of monopolies), the interpenetration of industrial and financial capital, the disappearance of internal convertibility into precious metals, the organization of international monetary blocs—all these phenomena which figure in the analysis of imperialism have modified the rules of the money game and the relations between the internal and international conjunctures.

It remains true that the supreme purpose of this economistic ideology is to construct a general model of monetary equilibrium, completing the model of real equilibrium as constructed by Walras.

The method of historical materialism is the very opposite of that which is promoted by research directed toward general monetary equilibrium. This is so, not because it ignores monetary techniques and policies, but because it goes further, placing these techniques and policies in their setting, as instruments of the bourgeois state in the internal and international class struggle.

4. GROUND RENT

1. We know that Marx took over Ricardo's theory of differential rent. I have nothing to add here to the remark made by Benetti to the effect that this was not an example of "marginalist" reasoning.[1] Marginalism assumes that production varies through the association of increasing doses of one factor with another factor, whose quantity is fixed. Here, the same dose of total social labor (with the same proportion of direct and indirect labor) gives different results depending on the quality of the soil (which, not being homogeneous, is therefore not a factor). Marx, too, as we know, developed the theory of differential rent in the same spirit, by introducing an intensive "Rent II" to complement the extensive "Rent I." By so doing he showed himself to be aware that fertility is not something natural, but results from the labor invested in what may be called "the production of soil"—a fact well known to agronomists and to everyone familiar with country life, but continually overlooked by economists, both classical and neoclassical.

It is hard to deny that differential rents exist. But the explanation that they are determined by the difference between the productivity of labor on a given plot of land

and the productivity of labor on the worst plot has not always carried conviction. An author who claims to be Marxist, Henri Regnault, has tried to build a theory of rent based upon the determination of agricultural prices by average conditions of production, just as in industry.[2] The good quality plot of land thus receives a positive differential rent, while the poor quality one (poor in relation to the "average" plot) receives a negative differential rent. The latter is possible only if it comes as a deduction from an absolute rent which is greater in amount. Differential rents are thus presented as resulting from transfers made from the owners of worse plots to the owners of better plots. On this basis Regnault proposes a reconsideration of the analysis of "external economies."

This is certainly a stimulating reflection. But what is truly the point of Marx's argument (and Ricardo's)? What worries Regnault is that, as he sees it, this argument brings in "demand" in a way that is unusual with Marx. I do not agree. I think that the argument is based on different grounds—namely, on whether or not the average conditions are reproducible. If the average conditions are indeed reproducible (crystallized in equipment which can always be acquired), then the capitalists receive super-profits—and not rents (not even monopoly rents)—which are positive or negative depending on whether they use equipment that is superior or inferior to the average. But if we are dealing with the natural conditions of production, that is, by definition, with conditions that are *not* reproducible (over and above the degree to which they may be modified, as is envisaged in Rent II), does not the concept of an "average" vanish?

However that may be, whether we are concerned with industry (reproducible means) or with agriculture (non-reproducible conditions), demand enters into the matter in both cases, and in the same way. When a productive system is given (and it matters little here whether it be expressed in values, as with Marx, or in prices, as with Ricardo and Sraffa), this presupposes that production is adequately adjusted to demand: the quantitative distribution of the production in excess of productive consumption needed between each product 1 ..., i ..., n, corresponds to an equivalent distribution of demand between wage earners and capitalists (including in this the demand resulting from the expanded reproduction). Marx does not eliminate use-value and does not fall into a way of looking at things that is based one-sidedly upon exchange value.

2. However, what interests us here is absolute rent, that which is paid for the worst land (*not* marginal land). Marx relates the existence of such rent to that of a class: the landowners.

Is the level of this rent determined? If so, why and how? Marx might have used an argument here similar to his argument about interest, saying that absolute rent is indeterminate and results from the confrontation of two classes, the landowners and the capitalists, with merely a floor—zero— and a ceiling—a level of absolute rent which absorbs all the surplus value.

Why not? For we know that rent is a category of distribution, since the landowner plays no part in the process of production. Obviously, each of these two forms of transfer income has its own status: if the landowners were to refuse to lease their land then no production could take place, whereas, if money were to disappear, it would be re-created. The soil forms part of the *natural* conditions of production; money is one of its *social* conditions.

Apart from that, though, the same argument could be advanced. It would incur the same criticism, namely, that the floor is too low (with zero rent the land would no longer be made available for renting) and the ceiling too high (if rent absorbed the whole of surplus value, the capitalists would stop producing).

The question seems to be, then: Is rent determined by some economic law which forms part of the whole system of laws governing price formation, or by a pure and simple relation of power? Actually, this question is badly put and needs to be replaced by another: How does this class struggle (between landowners and capitalists) operate on a given economic basis and how does it modify that basis? Only thus will the two domains, that of economics and that of the class struggle, not be separated but be taken together, so defining, here as elsewhere, the true domain of social science: historical materialism.

Yet Marx here gives a simple answer to the question of how rent is determined, one that refers to economic reality only. He affirms that it is the difference in the organic composition of capital, which is lower in agriculture, that determines the value retained by the landowner. I have already said that I find this proposition unacceptable,[3] both on the empirical plane (is the organic composition in agriculture always lower? why so? and if it were *higher*, should the rent be negative?) and on the plane of logic—even if the organic composition were higher in agriculture, could not the rent imposed by landownership act so as to distort prices (as compared with prices of production without rent), just as competition between capitalists distorts prices of production (as compared with values)? In that case, though, are we slipping into indeterminacy?

3. So far as I know, only one writer, Regnault, attempting to substitute a different economic determination for that offered by Marx, has tried to link rent with the rate of interest. This is his key argument, presented in the form of an imaginary discourse:

"You own the capital, I own the land. You can take a lease

of my land, while I can borrow your capital, in return for paying the rate of interest. If you invest 100, you will gain $100r$ (r being the rate of profit). If I borrow 100, I gain $100(r - i)$. For the lease of my land I require you to pay me $100(r - i)$."

Regnault concludes that absolute rent results from the existence of a capital market wherein the rate of interest is lower than the average rate of profit. He also notes that this determination must not be confused with the determination of the price of land by capitalizing the rent.

What worries me here is that the capitalist who agreed to pay a rent equal to $100(r - i)$ would no longer be making the average profit r. Why, then, should he choose to invest in this branch, if he cannot add the average profit to his costs of production? Why should he agree to give up his status as a capitalist (receiving r) and be satisfied with that of a money-lender, receiving $r - (r - i)$, that is, i? Though the problem has been shifted back, it is still there.

4. Most Marxists who have concerned themselves with the question of rent—among those who are not content merely to expound what Marx wrote—have inclined toward indeterminacy on the economic plane, after rejecting determination by comparative organic composition. This is the case with Berthomeiu,[4] who, in this field as in others, has devoted himself, with Benetti and Cartelier, to showing the limitations of economic science. He has demonstrated quite rigorously that all we can deduce from a Ricardian, neo-Ricardian, or Sraffian system into which absolute rent has been introduced (which Ricardo refused to do, but which, as we see from Marx, can be done) is that rent and profit are inverse functions one of the other. I agree with his conclusion that economic theory cannot explain the *level* of this rent—cannot tell us what determines it.

It seems, indeed, undeniable that the levy upon the net

product constituted by absolute rent modifies relative prices and reduces the rate of profit, just as an increase in wages does. (We know that relative prices and the rate of profit depend on the level of wages.) This fact can be proved by using either Marx's transformation schemata or a Sraffian model.

Let us take, for example, a transformation schema with two branches (1) and (2), a rate of surplus value of 100 percent, and different organic compositions. Without absolute rent, the transformation schema, in the case of the illustrative example set out in the table below, gives a rate of profit of 28.5 percent and prices $p_1 = 38.5$ and $p_2 = 51.5$.

	Constant capital (1)	Variable capital (2)	Surplus product Form: Surplus value (3)	Form: Profit (4)	Values (5)	Prices of production (6)
Branch (1)	20	10	10	8.5	40	38.5
Branch (2)	30	10	10	11.5	50	51.5
Total	50	20	20	20	90	90

If, now, we assume that branch (1) has to bear an absolute rent of 4 (in value $\rho = 4$) for an average rate of profit proportional to capital advanced (30 and 40 respectively), we have:

Branch (1) $p_1 = 30(1 + r) + 4(\rho = 4)$

Branch (2) $p_2 = 40(1 + r)$

and: $p_1 + p_2 = 90$

which gives: $p_1 = 40.9, p_2 = 49.1$, and $r = 23$ percent.

There is, of course, no reason why the levy represented by absolute rent should be determined in advance and in value terms. All that can be said is that, if it exists ($\rho \neq 0$), then, on the one hand, it entails a modification of relative prices and of the average rate of profit, and, on the other hand, its magnitude could be defined in real terms, like wages, as a function of the prices themselves, in the general form:

$$\rho = \alpha p_1 + \beta p_2$$

It is also possible, of course, to include rent in a Sraffian schema (as Berthomieu has proposed) and arrive at the same conclusions. Absolute rent expresses a social relation and cannot be determined by a simple, natural economic law.

It seems to me, however, precisely for that reason that this critique stops just at the point where the problems start to become interesting. What I see as important is how rent is determined in the domain of historical materialism—for it is indeed determined in that domain.

Historical materialism, as has been said, cannot be reduced to a games theory detached from its economic basis. It is not a formal exercise enabling us to decide the point of equilibrium between two or three partners (bourgeoisie and proletariat, or these two classes plus the landowners) who are in rivalry over the sharing of a given cake. For the beginning of an historical materialist analysis of how rent is determined, I refer the reader to the works of Lipietz, Rey, Faure, Lautier, and myself.[5]

5. Before turning to the last mentioned analyses, however, I think it is relevant to recall that Marx already replied to this problematic in his own way, both in *Capital* and in some other, "political" writings.

After determining rent by comparative organic composition, Marx moves on, and in the chapters that follow examines the history of rent. What does he do then? He forgets all about organic compositions, makes no further allusion to them, does not even try to give any indication of what they are. Moreover, he stops talking about landowners in general and speaks instead, when he is dealing with England, of "landlords," whom he counterposes to "farmers," and, when he is dealing with France, of "peasants." Here we enter right into the realm of historical materialism.

The case that Marx studies, that of England, is rich in lessons concerning his method, the way he determines rent in the realm of historical materialism. So long as the class of landlords shared power with the bourgeoisie in England (and here we see once more the state intervening in order to widen the "economic" domain), a high rent cut off part of profit. This rent was determined by the division of labor between agriculture and industry which had to be maintained so long as the English economy was obliged to feed its workers without importing cereals (this being practically forbidden by the Corn Laws). It can be shown that, in order to meet the requirement of equilibrium of supply and demand for agricultural products, on the one hand, and industrial products, on the other, the economic system assigned a given level to rent. If it rose above that level, accumulation in industry would be slowed down and then the supply of grain would be greater than the demand. If it fell below that level, the opposite process would ensue.

This example shows that Marx did not exclude the structure of demand from his analysis, though he did not reduce this analysis to a "general equilibrium" à la Walras, which is merely a static description and—as an explanation—mere tautology. Marx transcends the problem by envisaging dynamic equilibrium. Rent, determined immediately by a confrontation between classes, operates on the basis of economic laws, of an economic reality in which equilibrium of supply and demand is inescapable.

We have seen how Marx integrates demand into the process of accumulation, and how the dynamic equilibrium of supply and demand for production goods and consumer goods is what closes the system, determining at one and the same time, on the basis of a given real wage (the value of labor power), the relative prices and the rate of profit. This first model comprised only two classes (proletarians and capitalists) and two forms of income (wages and profits). The closing of the system implied a certain distribution of labor power between each of the departments, I and II—that is, an adequate mode of division of labor, in conformity with the structure of demand.

Let us continue this same line of reasoning, after introducing absolute rent $\rho = f(p_1 p_2 \ldots)$. If the technical data of production (material inputs and inputs of direct labor) and the real wage (the value of labor power) are given, and if we know also what the rent is spent on (say, for instance, it is wholly spent on luxury goods), then for a given system there is only one level of rent that makes dynamic equilibrium possible. The position is the same, *mutatis mutandis*, as with wages. If the rent rises any higher than that level, then profit is reduced and growth slows, affecting the labor market so as to reduce wages. Conversely, if the rent falls below that level, this entails a crisis of realization: excessive profits foster an increase in production which cannot find an outlet, if the level of wages remains unchanged.

The model includes thenceforth three classes and three types of income. The struggles and alliances between these three classes operate on the basis of an economic system which is defined by adequate modes of division of labor, and in their turn, as we have seen where the two fundamental classes are concerned, these struggles and alliances modify the conditions in which the system functions.

The class struggles do modify this economic basis. How, in fact, did the English bourgeoisie succeed in reducing the rent charged by the landlords? By abolishing the Corn Laws and substituting for English wheat American wheat which paid no rent (since there were no landlords on the other side of the

Atlantic). It was thus by establishing a new alliance of classes (between English capitalists and American farmers) that the English bourgeoisie freed itself from its local adversary. In its turn, this redistribution of forces modified the division of labor. In England it made possible accelerated industrialization, and in American accelerated development of agriculture. On the scale of the entity "England–America," the economic laws of equilibrium between supply and demand reappear—"without rent."

When, in contrast to this case, Marx analyzes the case of France, he starts from the alliance between the bourgeoisie and the peasants. Here, there were peasants, who owned their land and their capital and exploited wage labor only marginally. Marx refrains from splitting the peasant into three beings—the landowner, the capitalist, and the proletarian—in the way that our neoclassical economists later presumed to do. Marx knows that what is involved here is a peasant mode of production articulated with and dominated by the capitalist mode. He knows that, in this peasant mode, production for subsistence remains important, but also that domination by capital compels the marketing of part of the product. The alliance between the bourgeoisie and the peasants (an unequal alliance, in which the bourgeoisie was in command, but an alliance nevertheless, directed against the proletariat) found expression in the agricultural policy of the French state (protectionism and other measures permitting agricultural products to be sold at a relatively high price). It may be that this policy resulted in the peasants' standard of living being higher than that of the proletarians—the comparison is difficult to make. But it is pointless to give the name of "rent" to the difference between the total income of the peasants (their subsistence plus what they got for the produce they marketed) and the sum of the counterpart of their labor and the reward of their capital. Here again, this alliance had "economic" effects, and it functioned on the basis of a division of labor which was different from that prevailing in England.

Gradually, as the proletarian danger retreated (after 1871, and with imperialist expansion) the bourgeoisie attached less importance to its alliance with the peasantry. It took steps to reduce agricultural prices and ended, though belatedly, by aligning the reward of peasant labor with the value of labor power. The stress laid by an entire line of research in France upon the "formal domination"[6] which deprived peasant proprietorship of its content (since this proprietorship no longer conferred the right to a pseudo-rent) finds here the objective conditions which have enabled it to develop systematically. Colonial settlement, and the social-democratic hegemony over the proletariat which accompanied it, facilitated this evolution. Benachenhou points out that settlement in Algeria benefited from the availability of "lands without owners" (owing to the laws expropriating the Algerians) and that Algerian wine, which paid no rent, made it possible to lower the income of French winegrowers.[7]

6. This line of analysis of rent seems to me to be alone capable of placing the problem of the determination of rent correctly in the realm of historical materialism.

From this standpoint the contribution made by Rey strikes me as being vital. We certainly owe to him the first systematic analysis of the determination of rent in terms of class alliances and of the articulation between the capitalist mode (proletarians and capitalists) and the feudal mode (peasants and landlords), together with the effects of this articulation upon the dominated feudal mode, transformed and subjected to the dominant capitalist mode. Rey's contribution is all the more important because he has shown how all this is related to the *world* capitalist system.

The work of Lipietz, which deals similarly with the problem of the determination of urban ground rent—a problem too long neglected by Marxists—also deserves mention, together with the more systematic developments concerning the formal domination of peasant farming by capital carried out by Faure, Lautier, and others.

As for my own contribution, I refer the reader to the chapter I have devoted to the subject in *L'Impérialisme et le développement inégal*. This contribution, mainly concerned with the articulation-cum-domination relationship between capitalism of the imperialist epoch and the peasant modes of the periphery, thus constitutes a transition to the next part of the present work, in which I seek to use the method of historical materialism as a tool for analyzing not the capitalist mode (and the central formations) but the world capitalist system (the central and peripheral formations in relation to each other).

5. THE IMPERIALIST SYSTEM AND THE DEVELOPMENT OF A WORLD-SCALE HIERARCHY IN THE PRICE OF LABOR POWER

1. At this point it is essential to turn from the capitalist mode and consider the worldwide capitalist system. Our answer to the questions, formulated in terms of historical materialism, regarding the articulation between class struggles on the world scale, on the one hand, and, on the other, the economic laws that seem to govern the functioning of the world economy (that is, the functioning of the law of value on the world scale or the laws of accumulation on the world scale), can and must be guided by the method Marx employed in dealing with the European capitalist formations of his own day.

In this shift (from the capitalist mode to the world scale capitalist system) lies the entire subversive power of Marxism in our time.[1] It is here also that we find Lenin's essential contribution: his revolutionary merit consisted in presenting the problems of historical materialism in terms of struggles within the imperialist system, and no longer merely within capitalism. I counterpose this view to the one predominant in the West, which emphasized chiefly some other aspects of Leninism (such as party organization) which seem to me to be secondary and derivative. Let me remind the reader of my fundamental thesis, that the obscuring of this change of focus testifies merely to the hegemony of social-democratic ideology (revisionism, either open or shamefaced) in the working classes of the West, and justifies us in speaking of a pre-imperialist tendency among Marxists.

2. The world system has a history, the history of its gradual formation. If we consider the system as we see it today, that is, in empirical-descriptive terms, its appearance is one of variety, heterogeneity, and complexity in the social formations that make it up. This diversity seems to rule out any attempt to construct general rules or laws (in the realm of economics *or* in that of historical materialism), because the questions seem to lie on such different planes that they are irreducible to a common base.

Under these conditions there is a strong temptation to opt for one or other of the two following attitudes: either we forget the class struggle and try to formulate economic laws for the functioning of the world economy, or else we deny that there can be any laws valid for the world economy, and take refuge in the language of world politics, in which it seems easier to describe how a great variety of class conflicts and class alliances are interrelated on the world scale. In the first case, the principal magnitudes characteristic of the world system (the relative prices of commodities exchanged on the international plane, the rates of profit in this area and that, the prices of labor power, the ground rents and mining rents, the incomes of the various classes, peasants and others, and so on) seem determined by objective laws of the economic kind. In the second case, on the contrary, it is indeterminacy that prevails, and we are called upon to engage in an exercise of "pure politics"—the counterpart of "pure economics"—in the nature of games theory.

My method seeks to mitigate both of these dangers. I aim to determine the magnitudes in question in the domain of historical materialism (just as Marx determined the magnitudes of the central capitalist mode in this domain). Just as Marx studied these determinations as transformations of values in the capitalist mode, so do I study them as transformations on the world level—that is, as the result of manifold determinations, situated on various levels of abstraction; as the synthesis of these determinations, the transformed form of the law of value which is the fundamental law of the whole system. Can these transformations be formulated in a particular algebraic form? Yes and no.

3. The world system does not seem to lend itself to formalization in algebraic terms. It is, in fact, made up of segments which appear heterogeneous and even incongruous: groups of frankly capitalist firms producing commodities by means of more or less efficient techniques and employing wage labor at various rates of real remuneration; zones which seem to be precapitalist, where products, not all of which are marketed, are produced in the setting of various peasant modes, with or without extortion of surplus labor in various forms (ground rent, tribute, and the like); groups of natural resources (minerals), access to which is more or less obstructed, depending on the laws of the states concerned—on whether or not they appropriate these resources. Furthermore, no world economy can be analyzed without considering the states; these exist not only on the plane of political reality but also on the economic plane. The economic exchanges between these states have to balance, there are national monetary systems, some of these are linked with others, and so on.

Any attempt at translating this set of realities into a system of equations seems to be a long shot. Even summing up a system regarded as being close to a pure capitalist mode in a model, whether Marxian (with Department I and Department

II expressed in values) or Sraffian, constitutes a simplification which must be surrounded with many precautions.

I do not think, however, that resort to relatively simple schemata must be ruled out. Each of these schemata will possess some value, not merely pedagogic but even scientific (even though such value is necessarily limited)—provided that we define precisely what data we are using, and realize what these data signify.

Here is an example. One can define a system in which commodities $1 \ldots, i \ldots, z$, are produced, some by means of techniques characterized by material inputs A_{ij}^c and quantities of direct labor L_i^c, and others by means of other techniques characterized by inputs A_{ij}^p and quantities of labor L_i^p. This system can be characterized as follows: (a) a single rate of profit r, the only regulator of distribution thoughout the system; (b) a single price P^i for each product i; (c) two different wage levels W^c and W^p ($W^c > W^p$). Certain commodities (l to m) have, under these conditions, a lower price if they are produced with techniques ($A_{ij}^c L_i^c$), others (n to z) with techniques ($A_{ij}^p L_i^p$), it being understood that those produced according to the first formula pay the wages W^c, and the others pay the wages W^p, and that in every case the capital receives the same reward r.

This system might illustrate (without explaining) the conditions of reproduction (equilibrium between supply and demand, and so on) in a model reflecting a certain reality, namely: (a) all products are world commodities (these commodities have only one price—that which is obtained under the conditions that make it the lowest); (b) capital is mobile on the world scale; (c) labor is *not* mobile, and obtains different rewards at the center and at the periphery. In other words, it is a schematization of the way the production process has been turned into a world process in the imperialist epoch.

A model of this kind can be expressed either in Sraffian

terms or in terms of value. This is what I suggested in *L'Echange inégal et la loi de la valeur*.[2] It is not a substitute for historical materialism, any more than the schemata in Volume II of *Capital* are. But it is useful because it makes explicit what seems to be an objective economic law in such a system, and therefore a basis upon which historical materialism can operate.

4. Faced with a formulation like this, three attitudes can be taken. The first consists in refusing to examine it, on the pretext that this is not historical materialism ("Where's the class struggle?"), together with sarcasms along the lines of: "Aha, here comes the theory of the center and the periphery, the ideological expression of the Third World bourgeoisies!" And so on. Never mind. What really worries those who take this attitude is the conclusions that will emerge.

The second attitude consists in succumbing to one's own invention, imagining that this *illustrative* model provides an *explanation*. That is the mistake made by the economists.

If we accept the data of the system and try to stay within its framework, we are obliged at the outset to ask three questions: (1) why, in the peripheral zone, do they not combine the techniques $A_{ij}^c L_i^c$ with the wages W^p, which would give a higher profit than can be got with the techniques $A_{ij}^p L_i^p$?; (2) why, in this case, doesn't all capital migrate from the center to the periphery?; (3) at a given moment, the distribution of techniques being what it is, is the international division of labor that results from it (the center specializing in branches of production l to m, the periphery in n to z) compatible with equilibrium in exchange, since the fractions of products l to m exchanged for products n to z, at prices pi, ought to be equal?

Economic theory endeavors to answer these questions, and fails. I have examined the various theories produced to explain the equilibrium of the balances of payments (theories of price effects or exchange effects), have shown the circular character of these arguments (based on the quantity theory of money or on assumptions regarding elasticities of demand which presuppose the result), and have concluded that they amounted to nothing more than an expression of the ideology of universal harmonies.[3] But when economic theory, turning away from these nonsensical notions, speaks of "reequilibrating" income effects, it hits the nail on the head. By so doing, however, it invites us to ask the real questions, which lie outside its own field: How are the structures adjusted to each other—that is, by the effect of what forces does this adjustment take place? (What is involved here is the class struggles on the world scale.)

The third possible attitude, therefore, is to ask the questions that arise at the frontiers of what the model gives us. This is my own attitude.

5. But before we come to analysis in terms of historical materialism, let us get what we can from the model. This model illustrates one possible case: the case in which labor is not exploited uniformly—that is, when the rates of surplus value are unequal. In order to introduce this hypothesis (it is, at this stage, no more than a hypothesis) we need to construct the model in terms of values, rather than directly in price terms. This is why I have dealt with the problem in this form, as Marx deals with it in Volume II of *Capital*, and not in Sraffa's form.

In the first place, this hypothesis is a possible one: there is a system of dynamic equilibrium of supply and demand that corresponds to it. Second, unequal exploitation is manifested in unequal exchange. All those who, rejecting unequal exchange, rush to raise the cheap argument that this is a matter of circulation, not production, either are not acquainted with the thesis in question (the root of the matter lies in the different conditions under which labor is exploited), or prefer to evade the thorny question of imperialist exploitation.

Third, unequal exploitation (and the unequal exchange which results from it) dictates inequality in the international division of labor. It distorts the structure of demand, accelerating autocentric accumulation at the center while hindering dependent, extroverted accumulation in the periphery. My model of accumulation at the center and in the periphery is intended to show how this happens.[4] It therefore reproduces the conditions of unequal development. It explains that the underdeveloped countries are as they are because they are super-exploited and not because they are backward (or, if they were indeed backward, that circumstance made it possible to super-exploit them). This is, in my view, the only correct Marxist thesis, any contrary one being merely an apologia for imperialism which boils down to the bourgeois thesis of "stages of growth."

Practical experience confirms this view. All the analyses and projections elaborated either by me (for Egypt, the Maghreb, Black Africa) or others have yielded the same result: all plans for a dependent development policy worked out in constant prices lead to blocking by double deficit, in the external balance and in the public finances; all plans for such a policy worked out *ex post*, at current prices (relative prices of imports and exports) lead to this same blockage occurring even sooner. There is only one explanation for this, namely, that the price structures are distorted (through the effect of combined class struggles on the world scale) so as to aggravate exploitation in the periphery.

Fourth, the model does not imply that the openly capitalist form of exploitation becomes general throughout the system. The system merely assumes commodity production, and that the commodities produced are world commodities. Although introducing a rate of profit r in each equation corresponding to a particular branch of production suggests a generalization of the capitalist form, that condition is not necessary for the logic of the model. We could, for example, retain the rate r for branches of production n to s while excluding it for branches t to z. That would mean that commodities n to s, produced in the periphery, are produced by the capitalist enterprises (and in this case we could also introduce here techniques $A_{ij}^c L_i^c$, with the rate of wages W^p), whereas commodities t to z are produced by noncapitalist modes but are subjected to capital through their integration in the market. Here we come upon "formal domination." It is easy to show that, in this case, the amount of surplus labor appropriated by the dominant capital is even larger—that is, the super-exploitation is still greater.

6. Now we can (and must) go beyond the model, which continues to be economic in character. Now, correctly, we bring in the class struggles.

Going beyond the model means, first, taking into account the historical origins of the system. This implies that we are able to define and analyze the precapitalist modes, to observe and analyze the effects of capital's domination of these modes, and so on. Contributions such as those made by Frank, Rey, and myself are meant to serve this fundamental purpose. In no case, though, are they more than beginnings. In this sphere, where very little work has so far been done, there is a need for partial, even daring, theses. The discussion has divided us and will go on dividing us, but the progress we are making is clear, because the anti-imperialist problematic is common to us all.

Going beyond the model means, second, appreciating that there are no economic laws that are independent of the class struggle. This is why I have declared that there can be no economic theory of the world economy.[5] For this reason too, I believe, Marx did not write his chapter on the world economy. Nevertheless some writers, homesick for economics, try to construct such a theory. To this category belong the authors of studies on the multinational corporations and those who talk of how "the process of production is being made worldwide." American radicals have made a useful contribution in this domain, although the problem they claim to solve is, in fact, insoluble. For, just as one cannot understand the capitalist mode on the basis of empirical observation of reality at the level of the capitalist enterprises (where what appears is prices and profits, not values and surplus value), one cannot understand the world capitalist system on the basis of empirical observation of the mutinational corporations.

Going beyond the model thus means trying to interrelate the class struggles on the world scale, and to make this interrelation operate on an economic base, explaining how these struggles modify this base, in what direction, and so on. This is what I am trying to do, and this is undoubtedly the essential contribution furnished by the Marxists of the Third World—which is, as a rule, poorly understood and badly received in the West. Without repeating all these analyses here, let me recall that I make distinction between: (a) the imperialist bourgeoisie which dominates the system as a whole and concentrates to its own advantage a substantial proportion of the suplus labor generated on the world scale; (b) the proletariat of the central countries, which enjoys increases in real wages more or less parallel to increases in the productivity of labor, and, on the whole, accepts the hegemony of social democracy (these two phenomena are interlinked, resulting from the historically completed structure of capitalism with autocentric accumulation, and are bound up with imperialism); (c) the dependent bourgeoisies of the periphery, whose place is defined by the international division of labor, and whose anti-imperialist activity modifies this division; (d) the proletariat of the periphery, subjected to super-exploitation by virtue of the incomplete character of the capitalist structure, its historical subordination (its extroverted type of accumulation) and the disconnection derived from this between the price of its labor power and the productivity of its labor—and which, consequently, is the spearhead of the revolutionary forces on the world scale; (e) the exploited peasantries of the periphery, sometimes subject to dual, articulated exploitation by precapitalist forms and by capital, sometimes directly exploited by capital alone, through formal subordination—thus always super-exploited, and as a result the proletariat's principal potential ally; (f) the exploiting classes of the noncapitalist modes, organized in relation to the foregoing.

This extremely simplified presentation illustrates the fact that the principal contradiction, that which governs all the others and the vicissitudes of which largely determine the objective conditions in which the others operate, is the one which counterposes the peoples of the periphery (the proletariat and the exploited peasantries) to imperialist capital—and not, of course, as some have tried to make me out as saying, the periphery as a whole to the center as a whole.

In the first place, these struggles determine directly and simultaneously the relative prices at which exchange takes place between center and periphery, and the structure of the international division of labor. They determine the orientation and the pace of accumulation at the center, in the periphery, and on the world scale. They thereby condition the struggles waged at the center.

These struggles take place in a domain defined by contrasts and alliances that change from one phase to another. The social-democratic alliance (hegemony of imperialism over the working classes at the center) is a constant all through the imperialist phase, except for possible moments of crisis when it can no longer function. Leadership of the national liberation alliance (of proletariat, peasantry, and at least part of the bourgeoisie) is disputed between the proletariat (in which case the entire bourgeoisie goes over to the enemy) and the bourgeoisie (which then succeeds in making imperialism accept new forms of the international division of labor).

These struggles and alliances thus determine: (a) the rate of surplus value on the world scale and the respective (differing) rates at the center and in the periphery; (b) the surplus labor extracted in the subordinated noncapitalist modes; (c) the price structure of the world commodities by which this surplus value is redistributed (and, in particular, is shared out between imperialist capital and the capital of the dependent bourgeoisies); (d) real wages, on the plane of their world average and on that of their averages at the center and in the periphery respectively; (e) the amount of rent drawn by the noncapitalist classes (especially in the periphery); (f) the balance of exchange between center and periphery; (g) the flow of commodities and capital (and consequently the rates of exchange); and so on.

The framework of analysis in terms of historical materialism on the world scale implies that we appreciate the worldwide character of commodities (and therefore of value) and the worldwide mobility of capital. These are only tendencies, of course, but they are essential tendencies, since they signify domination by capital on the scale of the system as a whole.

It is not the object of this work to discuss all of these questions. I shall take up only one of them, one that has hitherto been little studied—the question of mining rent.

6. THE THEORY AND PRACTICE OF MINING RENT IN THE PRESENT-DAY CAPITALIST SYSTEM

1. Does the Marxist theory of ground rent apply to the sphere of *mining*? Here we have the same situation of need for access to natural conditions of production, and of capital sometimes finding itself up against a barrier constituted by property ownership. However, mining presents some obvious special features.

The first of these is the nonrenewability of the resources to be exploited. This feature imposes a specific cost of production which does not enter into rent, namely, the cost of replacement. Under the capitalist system this cost is usually taken into account by the operator, the mining capitalist. But then this factor is determined by the conditions of capitalism's functioning, which means that it is limited in two ways: (1) by the time prospect of the capitalists' calculation of profit, and (2) by the time prospect of the concession by virtue of which they are allowed access to the resource in question. These two limits are usually not independent of each other. Mining capitalists therefore must be sure to put aside an amount sufficient to enable them to continue their activities, at the same rate of profit, when the mines they are working become exhausted. Thus, the mining capitalists devote part of their apparent gross profit (actually, this part is a cost) to exploration for new reserves, both in the area conceded to them and elsewhere. The relatively brief time prospect of the operation reflects the well-known fact that reserves are proportionate to output, and not vice versa: generally speaking, at any moment in history, reserves seem to be sufficient to satisfy no more than a score of years of exploitation.[1]

The cost of this exhaustion of resources for the community is quite different. I have already stated my view that mastery of social development by society itself implies a considerably longer time prospect than that of capitalist calculation, the rationality of which appears, in this respect, to be relative and short-term.[2] When, for example, society grants a concession by an act of state, the problem presents itself like this: when the resource becomes exhausted, the amount set aside for replacement must be adequate to have enabled an investment to be made which is sufficient *either* for a new mine of the same product to be exploited at the same social cost, *or* to substitute for this natural product an artificial substitute of the same use-value and with the same cost, *or*, finally, to replace this resource by another productive activity, in another domain (providing different use-values) but regarded as equivalent (that is, producing the same added value).

Some questions still remain open: (1) the uncertain character of such calculations (over a period of fifty years, for instance), an uncertainty which cannot be eliminated in any society, even a socialist one; (2) the problem of how, this being so, a classless society can technically rationalize its collective choices.

Is it necessary to add that this calculation goes beyond the question (which is insoluble anyway) of "external economies and diseconomies"? These factors may be allowed for to some extent under capitalism, by means of legislation imposing compensatory taxes.

Is it necessary also to add that nonrenewability is less peculiar to mineral production than it may seem? Cultivable soil is not inexhaustible, either, unless it be properly maintained; and the historical experience of capitalism shows, in this case too, how limited is its rationality (the irreversible wastage of soils under capitalism, especially in the periphery, is a fact of history). But there is more to it than that: resources which appear to be inexhaustible (air and water) need—when a certain degree of intensity of industrialization has been reached)—to be maintained in the same way as the soil, as has recently been discovered in connection with what is known as the problem of the environment.[3]

The second specific feature of mineral production is of a historical order. Mineral production appears and develops with the development of capitalism, whereas agricultural production, of course, predated capitalism. Capitalist ground rent grafted itself onto a preexistent category, but mining rent had practically no connection with any antecedent. Apart from that fact, however, the sphere of mining presents no special features at this stage.

One observes, therefore, in this domain as in that of agriculture, the phenomenon of differential rents. To be sure, these rents find specific forms of expression in mining. The heavy technology employed in mining emphasizes rents of type II (connected with intensification of investment) rather than those of type I. The obstacle to entry into this sector which is constituted by the amount of capital needed causes the differential rents frequently to be combined with monopoly super-profits (in the vulgar sense of the expression) of the sort known as "technological" (which may or may not be temporary) that ought not to be confused, conceptually at least, with rent.

Absolute mining rent sometimes makes its appearance over and above these costs, differential rents, and super-profits. It is at this level that, with respect to the conditions in which it is formed, determined, and spent, absolute mining rent offers analogies with, as well as specific differences from, ground rent.

2. Mining rent, like ground rent, appears when a particular social class controls access to the resources in question. The thesis I am putting forward here is that, in the world capitalist system, the class in question is none other than the bourgeoisie of the periphery—that is, that the formation of mining rent is conditioned by the emergence of this bourgeoisie.

Mining rent existed earlier, of course, at the center of the system. Whenever the owners of the soil also put to advantage their rights over the subsoil, they imposed a mining rent on the capitalist operators. An example of this is the rent charged for the oilfields of the United States (meaning the absolute rent paid to the owners of the poorest deposits, not differential rents, which are indeed appropriated by those companies which exploit the richer deposits—for example, the ones in the Middle East). Generally, though, in the domain of mining, the capitalist state, acting in the name of the collective interests of the bourgeoisie, while asserting a right of ownership over the subsoil, was satisfied with allowing the dominant sectors of capital more or less free access to these resources in return for merely symbolic royalties.

The same applied on the plane of the world system. Control by the imperialist states over the colonies, and even over states enjoying formal independence, had for a long time the corollary of free access for the monopolies to the natural resources of the periphery, as is shown by the gratuitous concessions granted by the colonial administrations or wrested by means of gunboat diplomacy, or else obtained by paying a mere symbolic royalty, a "baksheesh" falling into the category of capital's overhead costs rather than rent.

Mining rent has emerged in recent times, on the plane of

the world system, when the states of the periphery have begun trying to impose a real royalty for access to the resources of the Third World. We perceive at once that the conditions for the emergence of the class with which the formation of mining rent is connected are different from those which apply to ground rent. The bourgeoisie in question was not "engendered" by mining rent; it originated elsewhere—in the process of the development of industry for import substitution, in the second phase of imperialist development. This bourgeoisie made itself felt through its collective instrument, the state.

At the conceptual level we must distinguish clearly between the *rentier* state and the capitalist firm exploiting the minerals, whether this be foreign or native, even if, in the latter case, it be a state-owned firm. Since the product in question is exported, the conditions of its exploitation, making possible a profit for the operating capital as well as a rent, are determined by the confrontation, on the world scale, between the states which own the resources and the monopoly capital which dominates the mining activity.

These monopolies are, of course, no more in the position of farmers in agriculture than the states are in the position of landlords. The analogy has its obvious limitations. The superficial formulation of the neoclassicists would speak here of "bilateral monopoly," in contrast to the "pure and perfect" double competition of the farmers and landlords. I prefer to avoid this sort of formal analysis and to describe instead the classes engaged.

3. At this point we need to ask how the level of mining rent is determined. Here again we cannot be satisfied with a "spectrum theory" which states that this rent is situated between zero and the level at which it would absorb the whole of the world surplus value.

My thesis is that the level of this rent is determined by the structure of the international division of labor, and in its turn modifies this structure. It is in these terms that I provide an economic anchoring for this class struggle waged on the world scale. My thesis is closely linked with that concerning the phases of imperialism, the international class alliances associated with them, and the forms of the division of labor dictated by these alliances. To each phase there thus corresponds a certain simultaneous arrangement of production and demand, an adequate structure of income distribution (a hierarchy of rewards for labor power, the level of profit and its distribution). Mining rent makes its appearance at the present moment in the crisis of the imperialist system—when, with the present structure of the division of labor, the surplus labor which capital as a whole extorts from the proletarians and peasants exploited in the system can no longer grow at a suitable rate. In other words, it appears at the moment when a resumption of accumulation requires that the cards be redealt and the division of labor modified.

Now we see how the level of this rent is determined: it is the level at which the rate of profit is maximized on the world scale through reestablishing equivalence between supply and expanding demand by enlarging the mass of labor exploited. Concretely, the transfer from center to periphery which this rent constitutes should enable accelerated accumulation to take place in the periphery, where the rate of surplus value is higher, and thereby to raise the average level of profit on the world scale. The necessary condition for this accelerated accumulation is access to the center for the periphery's industrial exports. It could then be shown that this transfer must promote a new equilibrium on the world scale, including a structural reequilibration of balances of payments, with the surplus being gradually absorbed by imports of equipment, payment of the profits of the center's technological monopolies, and so on. A determination like this is operative, of course, only on the world scale, and does not rule out the possibility of "imbalances" affecting certain periods and certain countries.

My thesis assumes as accepted that the present crisis is indeed a crisis of imperialism and that its principal origin does not lie at the center of the system but in the contradiction on the world scale in the relations between the center and the periphery.[4] This thesis is known to be unpopular in the West. It is based upon a preliminary analysis of the structure of accumulation on the world scale, to which I refer the reader.[5] As a first approximation, I distinguish between three phases in the evolution of capital accumulation in the capitalist system.

During the first phase (from the end of the nineteenth century to the 1930s or 1950s, depending on particular countries and regions), the international division of labor, colonial in type, restricted the periphery to producing agricultural and mineral products destined for export to the central countries, which kept for themselves all the industries, both basic and light, including those which supplied the periphery's imports. This division of labor, based upon the class alliance between imperialism and the feudalists and compradors, entailed a structure of the relative prices of the commodities exchanged on the world level which favored to the utmost the accumulation of industrial capital at the center of the system. This accumulation was based upon the principal markets existing at the center and the secondary market available in the periphery, importing manufactured consumer goods. The central markets gradually grew with the rise in wages at the center parallel to the development of the productive forces, whereas expansion was restricted in the periphery by stagnation in the reward of labor and by the unequal exchange in which this was manifested. In turn, unequal exchange hastened the rate of expansion at the center. Under these conditions, the dynamic equilibrium of overall supply and demand reproduced an increasing gap between center and periphery—that is, it simultaneously reproduced capitalist development and capitalist "under-development."

The price structures corresponding to this dynamic equilibrium included ground rents which rewarded the landowners allied to imperialism, but not mining rents; the capital of the imperialist monopolies reserved the right of free access to the resources of the periphery's subsoil, confining the bourgeoisie of the dominated regions to a comprador role.

The second phase of imperialist development can be characterized as that of industrialization of the periphery for import substitution. This phase, which has occupied the last twenty-five years, assumes a recasting of the international class alliances, with the national bourgeoisies taking the place of the feudalists and compradors, as a result of a series of victories over imperialism won by the national liberation movement. During this phase the dynamic equilibrium has continued to operate mainly on the basis of expansion of the central market. This expansion was fed by increases in wages and accentuated by the maintenance of unequal exchange, with the periphery continuing to supply raw materials (under conditions of stagnation or even decline of the rewards of labor), with which it now paid for imports of industrial equipment goods instead of the consumer goods imported hitherto.

The price structures corresponding to this phase still did not include mining rents, since the capital of the imperialist monopolies succeeded in this period in retaining their free access to the subsoil of the independent Third World. On the other hand, ground rents disappeared in some cases when the alliance with the feudalists was broken through bourgeois agrarian reforms which established new classes of kulaks and middle peasants. The relative reduction in the prices of agricultural produce which ensued was to the advantage of the local bourgeoisie engaged in import substitution industry, just as it was to the advantage of imperialism insofar as the agricultural products in question continued to be exported to the center.

My thesis regarding the present crisis starts from this analysis of accumulation on the world scale during the period following the Second World War, and of the blocking of this process. One of the ways open for overcoming the fall in the rate of profit implied by this blockage was to revise the conditions of North–South exchanges. The inclusion of mining rents in the prices of the products of their natural resources exported by the countries of the South would improve the financing capacity of the periphery's bourgeoisie and enable it to enter upon a new stage of industrialization based upon the exporting of industrial products to the center. The shifting of certain industries from the North, by re-creating a reserve of unemployment, would at the same time enable the rate of profit to be raised. Expansion would then be initiated by the exporting industries of the South, on the basis of which new industries capable of leading the economy forward would be able to resume their expansion in the North.

This (completely capitalist) way of overcoming the contradictions of the world system constitutes the program of the bourgeoisies of the periphery, their "new international economic order." Although it is fully compatible with the maintenance, and even the development, of the imperialist system, it is nevertheless still rejected, because the monopolies are not able to impose upon the working classes of the center the restructurings implicit in a resumption of accumulation on the world scale on these new foundations. The failure of the negotiations between North and South was foreseeable, since for their success the working classes of the North would first have had to be defeated.

At the same time, if negotiations of this sort were to succeed, and a new international division of labor were to be established, it would mean the breakup of the apparent bloc of the Third World states, because of the highly unequal opportunities available to the different countries of the periphery for the imposition of mining rents and for using these rents to develop export industries. The breakup of the Third World into what are increasingly spoken of as "sub-imperialisms" (I prefer to call them imperialist relay stations) and reserve zones doomed to decrepitude (the "Bangladeshi-zation" of the "Fourth World," the famine in the Sahel, and so on) is implicit in this prospect which I have described elsewhere.

Understood in this way, the problem of the determination of rent, in the domain of historical materialism, is closely linked with the problem of how it is spent. While landowners are usually regarded as being an unproductive class (the renewal of their income, which is guaranteed by their owner-ship of property, allows them to devote this income to consumption), the peripheral bourgeoisie needs mining rent in order to finance its accumulation. The sphere of this accumulation is not the mining activity itself, or even the forward-linked processing industries, but the economy as a whole. The bourgeoisie of the periphery is thus a productive class, even though it is dependent and thus parasitic. The close relation here between the way the rent is spent and the way it is determined is merely one more manifestation of demand, which Marxism, contrary to an all too common view, does not exclude from its analysis.

Thus, my thesis integrates the theory of mining rent into historical materialism considered on the world scale. It links the determination of rent with the hierarchical structure of the rewarding of labor power on the world scale, and thereby with international class struggles and class alliances. In short, mining rent emerges because Algeria and Iran are industrial-izing themselves (even if only in a dependent way), and not vice versa.

4. The problem of substitutes is connected with this principal determination. It has been well observed that the price of natural resources cannot rise higher than that of the artificial substitutes for these resources. This common sense observation needs to be generalized: throughout the capitalist system the price of no commodity can rise above that of the commodity which can be substituted for it—that is, which possesses the same or similar use-value. I have stressed this point,[6] which demolishes the neoclassical attempt to base economics upon the irreducible character of use-values, whereas the latter are largely the product of society (though not exclusively, of course, since there is a natural basis which makes it impossible for drinking water to serve as a substitute for a coat, their use-values being too different). Coca-Cola and lemonade are two use-values which can quite well be substituted one for the other.

The existence of substitutes, whether close or remote, always gives rise to what have been called sectoral rents. This term causes confusion, because what is involved is, in fact, something different, connected with the ways in which the surplus is distributed. The surplus is generated collectively but is then distributed in accordance with many different determining factors, into which enter all the elements making up social life and the reproduction thereof. I shall come back to this very general conclusion concerning the relations between the economy (the generation and distribution of the surplus) and historical materialism. In any case, there is no shortage of examples from the sphere of mineral production which illustrate this sort of problem. What values (or prices) are being considered? Those of oil, or of energy? At what levels do the economic laws operate, then? At the level of the enterprise? Or of the branch of production? Or of the complex of branches? Or of the national economy? Or of the world economy? Is it possible to define the surplus product at each of these levels? Or do we have to define it first of all on the global level, and only then examine the laws governing its distribution?

The problem of substitutes and of price solidarities thus brings us to the more general problem of the more or less collective nature of surplus value in the capitalist system. Furthermore, of course, the appearance of mining rent modifies the structure of relative prices and the average rate of profit, just as ground rent does, and for the same reasons.

5. The preceding reflections were inspired by the recent history of rent for oil. But views very different from these have been put forward in connection with the rise in the price of oil after October 1973.[7] Some of these stress the objective conditions governing the production of energy: for example, the reversal in the trend of the relative cost of oil, which, after declining for a century, was said to have begun a long upward swing in the 1960s and 1970s. Others place emphasis on the interimperialist contradictions, pointing to the concern of the United States to turn back in its own favor a worsening situation (dollar crises, etc.), by mobilizing the multinational oil companies and the oil states against Europe and Japan. Some go even further and see in the collusion just mentioned an expression of the long-term strategy of the multinationals, which are said to have chosen to ally themselves with the states of the Third World against the central states, with the aim, through shifting the location of the industries they control, of raising their rate of profit. All these analyses, even when they seem to contain partial truths, commit the same fundamental economistic error of contrasting the multinationals (metropolitan monopoly capital) with the states of the center. They focus attention on circumstantial and secondary aspects, and classify the contradictions of the system erroneously, ascribing the determining position to the interimperialist contradiction or to that which sets the working classes of the West against the monopolies,

and refusing to allow to the contradiction between the peoples of the periphery, on the one hand, and the monopolies, on the other, the historical role as a driving force which I see it as fulfilling for the entire epoch of imperialism—refusing to see that it is *this* contradiction that produces, as a consequence, the (secondary) contradiction counterposing the dependent bourgeoisies of the periphery (and their states) to the monopolies (and their states). The source of this error is to be found in American radical writings directed against the multinationals.

I see in the oil affair, however, an early manifestation of a much more general tendency, which corresponds to the new strategy of the bourgeoisies of the periphery. The battle for the "new international economic order," the striving (though still weak) of the Third World states to create the means for a solidarity which would enable them to impose a substantial all-around rise in the prices of raw materials, testifies to the operation of this general tendency.

6. It is impossible, of course, to decide the question of how mining rent is determined in general and abstract terms. Like any other question, this one needs to be made the subject of concrete analyses of concrete situations. Specific circumstances govern the struggle for rent and its possible outcome in the case of each mineral. For comparison one could refer to the case of iron ore,[8] which was for a long time produced exclusively in the developed countries for use in their national iron and steel industries. Because the needs of these industries can no longer be satisfied by the big producers (the United States, France, and Sweden, to which we must add the Soviet Union), the West has provided itself with a "mining belt" made up of reliable countries (Canada, Brazil, South Africa, Australia) which can supply ore at competitive prices in quantities broadly sufficient for the foreseeable future. Under these conditions, the producers in

the Third World (Venezuela, Mauritania, Guinea, Liberia, Gabon, India, Malaysia) have been made "marginal" and deprived of bargaining power (especially if Brazil persists in declining to support them). On the other hand, the financial requirements for establishing iron and steel industries in the Third World are considerable—nearly $50 billion must be obtained within five or six years—and cannot be found either in the West or in the countries of the Eastern bloc. Here we see the possible emergence of an association of three partners: steel-producing countries of the Third World, countries with large financial resources (the members of OPEC, for instance), and the mining countries mentioned above. Such an association would strengthen the collective independence of the Third World and dissociate the iron mining and steel production of the periphery from the central set of states, whose domination effect is felt at present by both the mining and the steel-making countries of the Third World. In an association of this sort, mining rent would have to be negotiated between the separate states involved. It can be seen from this example, however, that the struggle over the price of the mineral itself is not the principal issue at stake in the battles that are now going on.

APPENDIX. ONCE MORE ON THE QUESTION OF TRANSFORMATION

1. What follows is not a new attempt to put forward a "solution" to the problem of "transformation." I believe, with Benetti, Cartelier, and Berthomieu, that Marx's critique of political economy was not a positive attempt to "correct and complement" Ricardo, but a critique of the very status of economic science, the nature of which was exposed by Marx—as "what the bourgeoisie has to say about its own practice," to use Benetti's phrase.[1] However, since fundamentally divergent viewpoints will probably continue on this issue among Marxists (meaning thereby all the trends that claim to be Marxist), divergent interpretations of transformation, its nature and implications, whether pertinent or not, will continue to be formulated by different writers.

I shall attempt the more modest task of trying to understand what it was that Marx did in Volume III of *Capital* and defending the view which I believe was his. I do not do this out of any sort of religious respect for the writings in question—have I not myself criticized Marx on the determination of rent, the indeterminacy of interest, and the tendency of

I wish to thank Andre Farhi, who kindly read through the first draft of this appendix and gave me the benefit of his comments.

the rate of profit to fall?[2] Have I not ventured to add something to what Marx wrote in the field of the theory of money and of the trade cycle?[3] However, I sense that what is involved here is a much more fundamental problem, one which concerns the very essence of Marxism.

In the first part of what follows (sections 2 to 8) I shall show:

(1) That value exists and that it can be calculated—that is, that commodities are indeed represented by quantities of total abstract social labor (direct and indirect), which constitute the common denominator (the standard), making possible comparison between them at a given moment, as well as over a period of time.

(2) That values are independent of the distribution of income between wages and profits.

(3) That prices, on the other hand, are not so independent, but that, once the value of labor power is known, prices can be related to values: that is, that transformation is legitimate and possible (one can improve upon Marx's first approximation without violating its spirit).

(4) That, within this framework, with the standard used being the quantity of abstract labor, Marx disregards the difficulties of the standard, in Sraffa's sense; that the conditions posited by Marx (equality of prices and values) define the choice of a unit of account [*numéraire*] (and not of a standard), in which what is involved is of very slight importance; that the choice of a different unit of account, gold, corresponding to historical reality, does not alter the essence of transformation.

(5) Finally, that values can be ascertained from prices and immediately visible empirical reality.

In (5) we come back to (1); the circle is complete, and value ceases to be a hazy, metaphysical, incalculable category—it is merely a category which, though precise (calculable), is not immediately obvious.

In the second part of what follows (from section 9 onward), I shall ask whether it is possible to do without the "detour through value" and remain satisfied with the immediate categories of price and wages. I shall then show:

(1) That this apparent "saving of time" raises the question of how to define a standard enabling us to measure the development of the productive forces.

(2) That Sraffa's attempt to define such a standard has failed.

(3) That, on the contrary, the value standard alone enables us to give a precise meaning and a reply to the question of how to measure progress in the productive forces—an obviously fundamental question.

2. I shall begin by recalling how value (the quantity of abstract social labor, direct and indirect, embodied in the production of a unit of a particular commodity) can be determined.

Let us assume a capitalist productive system producing two commodities, (1) and (2), both of which enter into productive consumption, the consumption needed for reconstituting labor power, and consumption by the capitalists. The physical quantities of (1) and (2) produced are each taken as unity, so that the productive and ultimate consumptions of these commodities are given, quantitatively, as fractions of unity. The total quantity of abstract direct labor is taken as unity, and is therefore assigned to the production of (1) and (2) in proportions the sum of which is unity.

For example, we have this system:

$$0.2v_1 + 0.4v_2 + 0.4 = v_1$$
$$0.5v_1 + 0.1v_2 + 0.6 = v_2$$

From this we deduce at once (without needing any hypothesis regarding the rate of surplus value) what the values are, namely

$$v_1 = 1.15 \text{ and } v_2 = 1.30,$$

which represent the total quantities of abstract labor, direct and indirect, needed to produce a unit of (1) and a unit of (2)—these physical quantities being known—with the unit of labor being the quantity of direct labor applied.

It will be helpful to make two observations at this point:

(1) The production of the two products (1) and (2) referred to here is concomitant. It is, for example, the production accomplished in year n. Nevertheless, it requires that the unit of direct labor mobilized has at its disposal a stock of 0.7 of a (physical) unit of product (1) and 0.5 of a unit of product (2). Whence do these means of labor originate? From a previous phase of production, that of year $n - 1$.

If the techniques of production in the previous years were the same as those of year n (stagnation of the productive forces) the following recurrent reasoning would be possible:

To produce one unit of (1) we need: 0.4 of a unit of direct labor, 0.2 of a unit of (1) and 0.4 of a unit of (2).

To produce 0.2 of a unit of (1) we need: 0.4 × 0.2 of a unit of direct labor, 0.2 × 0.2 of a unit of (1), and 0.4 × 0.2 of a unit of (2), and so on.

The sum $S = 0.2 + (0.2)^2 + \ldots = 0.25$.

The recurrent reasoning thus gives us this: it will be necessary to produce during the periods $(n - 4)$, $(n - 3)$, $(n - 2)$, $(n - 1)$ and n, 1.25 units of (1) with 0.4 × 1.25 of a unit of direct labor, 0.2 × 1.25 of a unit of (1) and 0.4 × 1.25 of a unit of (2). These are the same proportions as in the first equation of the system.

The same applies to the second equation of the system. This system of the series of years n, $n - 1$, $n - 2 \ldots$, thus gives the same values v_1 and v_2.

If, however, the techniques of production have progressed, we shall not consider the production formulas of the previous periods $n - 1$, $n - 2$ and so on, for the value transmitted by constant capital is not the value of the elements making up this capital in the periods $n - 1$, $n - 2$ and so on, during which they were actually produced, but their social value, that is, the value they possess in period n, today, since they can be reproduced under present conditions of production, which are more efficient.

When I constructed my model of balanced expanded accumulation, I was obliged, for this reason, to reckon the value of the products at the rate of the following period, the rate anticipated by the progress of the productive forces.[4]

Calculation of value does not dictate that of the historical values of the elements transmitted, but only the simultaneous solution of the present system of production.

This observation is useful insofar as it reminds us that there is no point in wandering off into a line of reasoning which goes back to the beginnings of history, in the way that, since Böhm-Bawerk, economists have commonly thought fit to do.[5]

(2) The values thus determined are rigorously independent of any assumption about distribution. There is no call to discover whether the producers dispose of all of the net product they produce, or are exploited.

3. However, the capitalist productive system is defined not only by its technical conditions (coefficients of inputs of means of production and inputs of direct labor); it is also defined by the value of labor power, which is the value of the

commodities necessary for reconstituting the latter. Let us assume that this is:

$$w = 0.2v_1 + 0.2v_2 = 0.50$$

The productive system thus possesses the characteristics listed below:

Total production	$1.0v_1 + 1.0v_2 = 2.45$
− Productive consumption	$0.7v_1 + 0.5v_2 = 1.45$
= Net product	$0.3v_1 + 0.5v_2 = 1.00$
− Value of labor power	$0.2v_1 + 0.2v_2 = 0.50$
= Surplus value	$0.1v_1 + 0.3v_2 = 0.50$

The rate of surplus value (100 percent) is identical in each branch the value composition of which is, according to Marx's formula ($c + v + pl = V$).

c		v		pl		V
$(0.2v_1 + 0.4v_2 = 0.75)$	+	0.20	+	0.20	=	1.15
$(0.5v_1 + 0.1v_2 = 0.70)$	+	0.30	+	0.30	=	1.30
Total 1.45	+	0.50	+	0.50	=	2.45

In this system will be recognized the magnitudes characteristic of Marx's analysis: the organic compositions (c/v) and the rate $pl/c + v$, so that

	pl/v	c/v	$pl/c + v$
(1)	100%	375%	21%
(2)	100%	233%	30%
(1) + (2)	100%	290%	26%

Here, then, we have our description of the productive system with two branches. The same would apply if there were n branches. It will be noted that my branches (1) and (2) have nothing to do with the Departments I and II of Volume II of *Capital*. My analysis is not concerned here with reproduction (simple or expanded), which is assumed to be insured by the overall structure of the productive system.

4. Marx's "first approximation" consists, as is known, of making the rate $pl/c + v$ an average 26 percent and, on this basis, distributing the surplus value (0.50) between branches (1) and (2) in proportion to the capital advanced $(c + v)$, so that here:

$$\begin{aligned}
&\text{profit (1)} = 0.24 &&\text{price (1)} = 1.19 \\
&\text{profit (2)} = 0.26 &&\text{price (2)} = 1.26 \\
&\Sigma \text{ profits} = 0.50 &&\Sigma \text{ prices} = 2.45
\end{aligned}$$

Is it possible to improve on this, while remaining faithful to the spirit of the method expressed in this "first approximation" of transformation attempted in Volume III?

Let us assume prices, as the transformed forms of values:

$$p_1 = x_1 v_1 \text{ and } p_2 = x_2 v_2$$

such that the surplus value is distributed in proportion to the capital advanced, at the rate of profit r.

We shall then have this system:

$$(0.2p_1 + 0.4p_2 + 0.4w)(1 + r) = p_1$$
$$(0.5p_1 + 0.1p_2 + 0.6w)(1 + r) = p_2$$
$$w = 0.2p_1 + 0.2p_2$$

It will be noted that, contrary to what we find in Sraffa,

here the value of labor power is integrated in the productive process as variable capital, and not treated as a category of distribution. The nominal wage w expressed in the price system p ensures that labor power is rewarded at its value.

The system is thus reduced to the two equations:

$$(0.28p_1 + 0.48p_2)(1 + r) = p_1$$
$$(0.62p_1 + 0.22p_2)(1 + r) = p_2$$

These two equations with three unknowns determine the system perfectly, within a factor of proportion—that is, they determine the rate r and the relative price p_1/p_2.

Actually, the system of these two equations enables us to express a relation between p_1 and p_2 independent of r, as here:

$$\frac{p_1}{0.28p_1 + 0.48p_2} = \frac{p_2}{0.62p_1 + 0.22p_2}$$

or:

$$62p_1{}^2 - 6p_1p_2 - 48p_2{}^2 = 0$$

in general form:

$$ap_1{}^2 + bp_1p_2 + cp_2{}^2 = 0$$

By assuming $p_1 = \alpha p_2$, we have a quadratic equation in α, here:

$$62\alpha^2 - 6\alpha - 48 = 0$$

which has two roots:

one negative

$$\alpha_1 = \frac{6 - \sqrt{11.940}}{124}$$

and the other positive

$$\alpha_2 = \frac{6 + \sqrt{11.940}}{124} = 0.93$$

The curve $ap_1{}^2 + bp_1p_2 + cp_2{}^2 = 0$ is thus a degenerated hyperbola, that is, two straight lines passing through the origin (when $p_1 = 0$, $p_2 = 0$ as well), of which one half-line is necessarily situated in the northeastern quadrant of the system of coordinates. This expresses the fact that the curve describes a relationship p_1p_2 which results from a real system of observed prices. Since a and c always have a different sign, $b^2 - 4ac$ is always positive. There is always a real solution, and only one. In other words, the relative price p_1/p_2 is determined, and r likewise.

In the case I have taken, for instance, if we select for our unit of account [*numéraire*] $p_1 = 1$, we have:

$$p_2 = 1.076, \quad r = 25.6\%, \text{ and } w = 0.41$$

The schema which has been developed here with two branches could be extended to n branches, with matrix algebra being used instead of illustration in two-dimensional space. This corresponds here to the conditions for validity of the Perron-Frobenius theorem.

In fact, the matrix form:

$$Ap = \frac{1}{1 + r} p$$

indicates that the vector p is determined to within a factor of proportionality.

5. The productive system thus described is therefore *closed*. Once the value of labor power (from which the rate of surplus is derived) has been given—that is, once the two equations given above have added to them an equation in the form $w = f(p_1, p_2)$—the rate of profit r and the relative prices are determined.

The choice of a standard is then actually the choice of a unit of account [*numéraire*]—that is, of a factor of proportionality, the true standard of the prices calculated in this way being value.

We should perhaps consider that Marx stipulates an additional condition, namely:

a—with prices and values equal, here:

$$p_1 + p_2 = 2.45$$

b—with profits and surplus value equal, here:

$$0.10p_1 + 0.30p_2 = 0.50$$

One or the other of these conditions would define a unit of account (a factor of proportionality).

It might be thought that there is some logic in choosing one of these two units of account rather than the other, since what is involved, according to Marx, is discovering how surplus value is distributed through competition between capitals. On this plane, Marx's second unit of account should be the one preferred.

These two units of account are equivalent to each other only in Marx's first approximation. Once this is left behind, since the two linear equations which define them are not homothetical, the solutions they give (the absolute prices) are different.

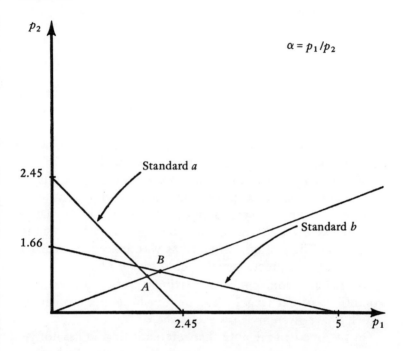

Whatever the unit of account—which has the general form $ap_1 + bp_2 = k$—the rate r is determined (here, 25 percent), as is also the ratio α (here, 0.93).

The unit of account (a), corresponding to equality between prices and values, here gives:

$$p_1 = 1.180 \qquad p_2 = 1.270 \qquad w = 0.490$$

The unit of account (b), corresponding to equality between profits and surplus value, here gives:

$$p_1 = 1.183 \qquad p_2 = 1.272 \qquad w = 0.491$$

But since the relative prices, like the rate of profit, are determined and independent of the unit of account, the difference made by whichever unit of account is chosen is very slight: all that this determines is the factor of proportionality.

6. The choice of unit of account is thus without any theoretical significance as regards the problem of transformation.

However, while the choice of unit of account may be arbitrary in economic theory, this is not so in the field of historical materialism. Prices are not constituted as relative prices but as absolute prices expressed in monetary units. Money is a fundamental category of commodity exchange, not a "veil," a "unit of account," introduced "subsequently."[6] The real unit of account was, indeed, a particular commodity, the precious metal—gold and/or silver.

Has the abandonment of convertibility radically altered the conditions of exchange? Here we touch upon a problem to which I have given my answer elsewhere.[7]

On the one hand, I note that reference to gold has not yet disappeared at the level of the world system. And can it disappear? I do not think so—not as long as the capitalist formations are not integrated into a single worldwide formation (on the political plane as on the others). I doubt whether such a super-imperialism makes sense. Theoretically, though, a world state form (Orwell's notorious *1984*) cannot be ruled out. But this would be something other than capitalism, while not socialism, as has been said.

On the other hand, I note that, at the level of the national formations, abandonment of internal convertibility does indeed alter the conditions governing the issue of money, by doing away with the internal "safety-net"—though not the external one.

7. Let me recapitulate my results.

If we accept the theory of value, that means accepting that prices and profits can be calculated as transformed forms of value. This proposition can be broken down as follows:

(a) A system of values can be transformed.

First, this operation can be carried out mathematically, since the productive system is defined by the inputs of constant capital (in physical technical coefficients) and direct labor (in physical quantity), on the one hand, and, on the other, by the value of labor power, prices can be derived from the original values.

Second, it is legitimate to do this. The only condition required is that concrete labors be reduced to abstract labor. Marx did this. Was he wrong, as seems to be the view, at least implicitly, of those who consider prices and values mutually incommensurable? I do not think so. Exchange does in fact reduce concrete labors to their common denominator: abstract labor. Besides, as Braverman has shown, the tendency of capital is, concretely, by taking the skill out of labor, to reduce it to the reality of abstract labor. On this point I do not go along with Benetti, Cartelier, and Berthomieu, who, in concluding that values and prices are incommensurable, go too far and throw the baby out with the bath water.[8]

Third, relative prices are independent of the unit of account; only absolute prices depend upon it. Whether one selects some arbitrary unit of account, or a unit of account corresponding to one of Marx's conditions, or the actual unit of account, makes very little difference.

What worries some people is that, in these results, r differs from the rate of surplus value. I think, though, that what would be inexplicable would be if it did *not* so differ: this would divorce the theory of alienation from its basis in reality.[9]

(b) Conversely, a given empirical system, characterized by

its prices, both absolute and, consequently, relative; its wage, both nominal and, consequently, real; its rate of profit; and its unit of account enables us to get back to the system of values in which it originates.

The empirical system in question presents itself to our observation, in fact, as a system of four equations (for two branches)

(1) $\begin{cases} \text{productive} \\ \text{system} \end{cases}$ $(0.2p_1 + 0.4p_2 + 0.4w)(1 + r) = p_1$
(2) $(0.5p_1 + 0.1p_2 + 0.6w)(1 + r) = p_2$
(3) wages $\qquad\qquad\qquad w = 0.2p_1 + 0.2p_2$
(4) unit of account $\qquad\qquad f(p_1 p_2) = 1$

which are verifiable because they are merely a formalization of immediate reality, p_1, p_2, w, r, and the unit of account being observed in the same way as the relations between them. Actually, we can read directly the system of values which lies behind this system of prices—it is this:

$$0.2v_1 + 0.4v_2 + 0.4 = v_1$$
$$0.5v_1 + 0.1v_2 + 0.6 = v_2$$

This gives us the original values, which are independent of distribution, whereas the prices are not.

Equations (3) and (4) do not concern us: we read directly from the productive system, (1) and (2), the coefficients which enable us to calculate the values. The parameters of this system are: tons of wheat and of iron and hours of direct labor. The solution of the system gives us hours of total labor, direct and indirect.

There is thus a one-to-one correspondence between the two systems.

This correspondence between values and prices signifies

that the value generated in the productive process can be distributed otherwise than one could deduce from consideration merely of this productive system itself.

This actual redistribution (the prices) results from a synthesis of several determinations, in this case three: (a) the structure of the productive system (including the rate of exploitation)—this is the fundamental determination; (b) competition between capitals—this is the second level characteristic of the capitalist mode; (c) the historical circumstances in which an actual unit of account has been imposed—these determine merely the factor of proportionality.

The true standard (what determines, in the last analysis) is thus *value*. The question of how this value is distributed, as the effect of what secondary determinations, is an essential one.

Marx answers this question in a way that is basically correct, though incomplete, in Volume III—which is, where this matter is concerned, as with rent and interest, a work that remained unfinished. But it was not a blunder on his part. His "first approximation" can be followed up with a more satisfactory calculation if this is desired—provided that one appreciates this calculation as what it is: an illustration of the answer to the question of how these multiple determinations operate so as to distort the essential, last analysis determination, and not a formal mathematical exercise.

The question of the distribution of value arose already within the capitalist mode: it arises *a fortiori* on the scale of the capitalist system.

Here, too, if we want to bring out what is essential, that is, the impact of the fundamental determination, illustrations by means of schemata formulated in value terms are more effective than pseudo-empirical illustrations formulated in prices. This is why I have chosen the former in formulating the laws of the world distribution of surplus value and surplus labor.

8. Furthermore, it is noteworthy that, in the case of a large number of products and under the actual conditions of production, characterized by the differences of organic composition we are familiar with, the price structure would differ very little from the structure of transformed values as Marx presents this in his first approximation. The differences are due much more to other circumstantial factors (monopolies, etc.). In fact, Marx's first approximation is adequate for practical purposes.

9. Whereas values are independent of distribution, relative prices, whether deduced from values by transformation or calculated directly, as Sraffa calculates them, are not.

Why, then, deduce prices from values, and not rest content with calculating them directly, without even raising the question of the values that correspond to them? Why this "detour through value"?

The answer is that value is irreplaceable as a standard. There is no other possible standard, since any other "standard" is elastic, varying with what it measures, and so not really a standard at all. It is not possible to consider that there is a cake "given" in advance which has to be divided: the nature of the cake depends on the way it is divided. On the other hand, the value standard enables us to define, in a precise and objective way, the development of the productive forces, which cannot be done by means of any other standard, which is always imperfect.

10. A system defined directly in price terms is also perfectly determined—in the sense that relative prices and the rate of profit are determined—once the rate of real wages is given.

But then there arises the question of a standard which Sraffa, in the Ricardian tradition, defines like this: is there a standard which would leave the net product unchanged while distribution (w or r) changed independently? The answer to this question is no. Let us see why this is so.

Sraffa does not analyze the system as Marx does. He excludes labor power from the productive process, in order to consider wages not as the value of labor power but as a distribution category. This is why he describes the system in the following form:

$$(0.2p_1 + 0.4p_2)(1 + r) + 0.4w = p_1$$
$$(0.5p_1 + 0.1p_2)(1 + r) + 0.6w = p_2$$

He further proposes, as we know, that we select as our standard the price of the net product:

$$0.3p_1 + 0.5p_2 = 1$$

With this standard, r and w are in a linear relationship which is independent of p_1 and p_2:

$$r = R(1 - w)$$

Here we check

a: that for $w = 1$; $r = 0$; $p_1 = 1.15$ and $p_2 = 1.30$

(the prices are here the values).

The system then becomes:

$$0.2p_1 + 0.4p_2 + 0.4 = p_1$$
$$0.5p_1 + 0.1p_2 + 0.6 = p_2$$
$$0.3p_1 + 0.5p_2 = 1$$

b: that for $w = 0$; $r = R = 70\%$: $p_1 = 1.22$ and $p_2 = 1.27$.

The system then becomes:

$$(0.2p_1 + 0.4p_2)(1 + R) = p_1$$
$$(0.5p_1 + 0.1p_2)(1 + R) = p_2$$
$$0.3p_1 + 0.5p_2 = 1$$

where the two first equations, combined, give:

$$5p_1^2 - p_1p_2 - 4p_2^2 = 0$$

With this standard, r and w are in a linear relationship described by the straight line shown in Figure 1, whereas any arbitrarily chosen standard gives a relationship between r and w which is neither linear nor monotonic (Figure 2).

But is this standard any better than others? Benetti and Cartelier have shown that it is not so at all: (a) because this standard presupposes Sraffa's treatment of wages: if the wage is integrated in the productive process as variable capital, the standard varies when w varies: it is no longer independent of prices; (b) because, even in Sraffa's formulation, since the net product changes with the passage of time (the result of growth), the standard is not independent of prices, but is elastic.

If then, we reintegrate w in the productive process, as we should, whatever the standard being used, we get three equations and four unknowns (p_1, p_2, r, and w). It is still possible to express r as a function of w, but the relationship is no longer linear, nor even of necessity a monotonic decreasing one (it is of the type shown in Figure 2).

11. The fundamental question underlying the dispute over whether to choose value as the standard, or something else, is that of how to measure, precisely and objectively, the progress of the productive forces.

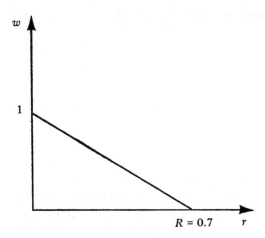

Figure 1

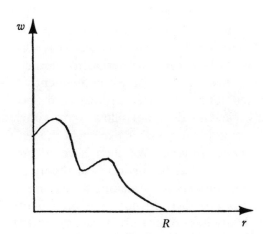

Figure 2

Let us assume two productive systems. The system of year O:

$$(a_{11}p_1 + a_{12}p_2)(1 + r) + waO_1 = p_1$$
$$(a_{21}p_1 + a_{22}p_2)(1 + r) + waO_2 = p_2$$

The system of year 1:

$$(a'_{11}p'_1 + a'_{12}p'_2)(1 + r) + w'a'O'_1 = p'_1$$
$$(a'_{21}p'_1 + a'_{22}p'_2)(1 + r) + w'a'O'_2 = p'_2$$

If the same standard is chosen for describing the two systems, we have a relation between w and r which is illustrated by one of three figures shown below (Figures 3–5).

Can we then compare systems O and 1 from the standpoint of the progress of the productive forces?

Sraffa's standard does not allow us to do this. In fact, the two curves can intersect, and one system is superior or inferior to the other depending on the standard chosen.

Besides, Sraffa's standard was not defined with this end in view. It was sought merely as a means of defining a distribution independent of prices. It solves this problem in a given system (condition of synchrony) but ceases to do so when the system evolves from one period to another (condition of diachrony). Even on this plane it consequently fails: the cake to be shared out has not been defined in advance.

Sraffa's standard does not allow us to conclude that one system is superior to another except in the exceptional case of homothetic progress. We then have Figure 6 (p. 104).

We know, too, that the neoclassical theory which takes up this question answers it by making the assumption of convex envelope curves which do not intersect (Figure 7, p. 104). But this theory has no scientific value, as Sraffa has shown. It implies the assumptions which enable it to arrive at the desired results: it is tautological.

12. The value standard, on the other hand, enables us to measure the progress of the productive forces from one phase to another; that was why Marx chose it.

It is not fair to Marx to reduce his proposition that value

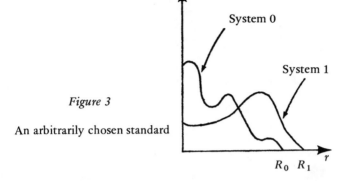

Figure 3

An arbitrarily chosen standard

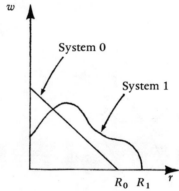

Figure 4

Sraffa's standard
deduced from system 0

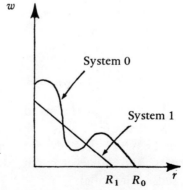

Figure 5

Sraffa's standard
deduced from system 1

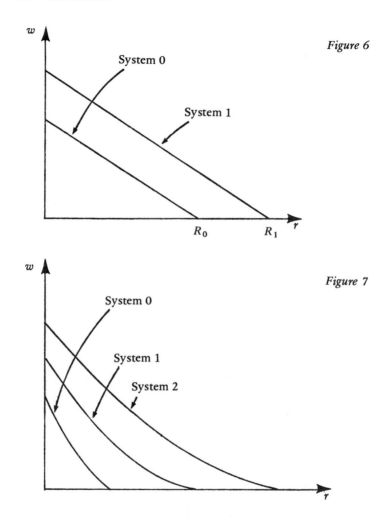

Figure 6

Figure 7

should be chosen as the standard of prices to the argument that this standard "works"—that is, that with it transformation is possible. The debate on transformation remains secondary, and, however much ink it has caused to flow, it is in no sense primordial.

Marx was actually seeking an instrument by which the development of the productive forces could be measured. This instrument is value. In fact, the quantity of socially necessary labor is, in the last analysis, society's only "wealth" —and value is independent of distribution.

This value standard means comparing the progress from one system (0) to another—(1), (2), etc.—along the Y-axis w. Along this axis $r = 0$, and wages w absorb the entire net product. The system which maximizes w for $r = 0$ maximizes income, or else minimizes the socially necessary labor time needed to produce a given amount of use-values. It corresponds, therefore, to more efficient, more highly developed productive forces.

Sraffa's standard, on the other hand, means comparing the systems along the X-axis r. For $w = 0$, $r = R$, and profit absorbs the entire product. The system which maximizes the rate of profit R will be considered the best. Isn't that the same thing? Not necessarily. The result of the two methods of comparison would be the same only if the curves (0) and (1) did not intersect. If they do intersect, then it is possible that the system which maximizes w does not maximize r.

Why is this? Because, along the Y-axis ($r = 0$) comparison between the systems takes into consideration simultaneously (for a system with two products) the four coefficients a_{11}, a_{12}, a_{21}, and a_{22}, corresponding to the commodity inputs, and the two coefficients a_{01} and a_{02}, defining the inputs of direct labor. The productive systems become (for $r = 0$):

$$a_{11}p_1 + a_{12}p_2 + waO_1 = p_1$$
$$a_{21}p_1 + a_{22}p_2 + waO_2 = p_2$$

and the prices p are then similar to the values.

If, however, we compare the productive systems along the X-axis for which $w = 0$, this means taking into consideration only the first four coefficients (production of commodities by means of commodities, and not by means of commodities plus direct labor) and leaving out the two coefficients of input of direct labor. The systems then become (for $w = 0$):

$$(a_{11}p_1 + a_{12}p_2)(1 + r) = p_1$$
$$(a_{21}p_1 + a_{22}p_2)(1 + r) = p_2$$

The value standard is superior because this standard alone considers production as the resultant of *all* the technical coefficients that describe it.

The conclusion of this analysis is fundamental: that social system which maximizes the rate of profit (for a given level of wages) does not necessarily maximize the development of the productive forces (the reduction of social labor time).

There is no way of doing without the theory of value. This theory alone enables us to link all the economic magnitudes (prices and incomes) to a common denominator—value, that is, the quantity of socially necessary labor—which is independent of the rules of distribution (exploitation, competition, and so on), and to do this both for characterizing a given phase (static synchronic analysis) and for measuring change from one phase to another (dynamic diachronic analysis) of the progress of the productive forces.

CONCLUSION.
THE GENESIS AND DISTRIBUTION
OF COLLECTIVE SURPLUS VALUE
IN THE IMPERIALIST SYSTEM

1. The arguments developed in the foregoing chapters were intended to define the nature of the "laws" which govern the genesis and distribution of the surplus labor extorted from the producers in the imperialist system of today.

Our results are situated, on the one hand, on the plane of method and, on the other hand, in the sphere of the application of method. According to the method, the genesis and distribution of surplus labor are not governed by economic laws, either simple or complex, but result from the class struggle, which operates, in the capitalist system, upon an economic basis which is itself an expression, in the last analysis, of the law of value. As for the sphere of application of this analysis in terms of historical materialism, it necessarily embraces from the very outset, in our day, the totality of the world imperialist system: analysis of the class struggle only has meaning (in the revolutionary sense, that is) if it is, first and foremost, analysis of the struggles and alliances between classes on the world scale, and only afterward analysis at the national levels subordinate thereto.

These are the lines of demarcation which separate the revolutionary interpretation of Marxism from its conservative interpretation, even when the latter is hidden behind a mask of dogmatism.

Marx himself defined, in his writings, the method of historical materialism, counterposing it to that of the bourgeois philosophies, both idealist (culminating in Hegel's expression of History as the realization of Reason, following on from the eighteenth-century Enlightenment) and mechanical-materialist (culminating in Ricardo's economism, which set up economics as a primary science).

Subsequently the European labor movement, far from developing further the revolutionary implications of Marx's break with the European (bourgeois) philosophical tradition, reintegrated into Marxism the various tendencies of this earlier philosophy. The return to Kant, interpreted as the "restoration" of the preeminence of the moral values of Progress and, on the other hand, an outgrowth toward a materialist search for laws common to society and nature (which, by way of Bogdanov, led to Soviet "Diamat"[1]), are signs of this reintegration. In this way there gradually took shape a "Western Marxism" which, by continuing (Western) bourgeois philosophy, caused Marxism to lose its truly universal bearing as the conception of a communist world.[2] This West-centered reduction of Marxism, not coincidentally, went along with the gradual formation of the imperialist system. The formation of the imperialist system did, in fact, damp down the class struggles at the center of the system by removing the major contradictions to its periphery.

Thereafter, the revolutionary interpretation of Marxism implied, of necessity, accepting the preeminence of the worldwide field of class struggle over the separate national fields. The line of demarcation dividing the revolutionary, Leninist-Maoist trend in Marxism from the conservative trend, now characterized by its pro-imperialist tendency, runs just there.

In this conclusion I propose to make these results more explicit and bring out their implications.

With regard to method, I claim that a correct appreciation of the dialectical relation between class struggle and economic base raises the question of the *collective* character of the way surplus value is generated. From this it follows that genesis and distribution of surplus labor (and, as regards distribution, understanding this in its true setting) are inseparable from each other. It is typical of dogmatic Marxism to separate them, in the name of a so-called anticirculationist argument which aims at justifying its pro-imperialist position. This is accompanied by an economistic position which reflects the integration of Marxism into the philosophy of bourgeois mechanical materialism. Both of these positions, which are inseparable, are characteristic of pro-imperialist West-centered Marxism (so-called Western Marxism) and lead to advocacy of the transcending of the contradictions of capitalism by the establishment of a new class mode of production, the statist mode. The revolutionary Leninist-Maoist trend is wholly committed to struggle against this bourgeois interpretation of Marxism.

2. In the capitalist system, then, class struggles operate on an economic base (determined in the last analysis by the law of value) and, by modifying this base, shape its evolution. History and theory are consequently inseparable.

The laws of historical materialism operate differently, of course, in precapitalist societies, since in them the economic field is transparent, and thus the relations between base and superstructure are not the same. The theory, which is still inseparable from history, does not have the same content. Likewise the mode of operation of "objective laws" which may exist in a developed classless society constitutes a problem of a different order, which has not been touched on. In my view it is too soon to attempt to define the nature of the social "rationality" of collective choices under communism.

Analysis in these terms of the reproduction of the system rules out any one-sided reduction—for example, to a "purely political relation of forces," or to a mechanical working of the law of value.

Class struggles shape the national and international division of labor and determine the objective conditions which are hidden behind immediate economic appearances—supply and demand. In its turn, however, the structure of supply and demand constitutes the objective basis on which these struggles take place.

When we postulate a "productive system" (schematizing a reality on a given scale, whether local, national, or worldwide), we simultaneously postulate a structure of demand. Marxism eliminates neither use-value nor demand, although it considers that exchange value dominates use-value. There is no lack of examples of demand making its appearance in the course of an analysis in terms of historical materialism. For example, the dynamic of growth requires that units of land and natural resources which are less and less "fertile" be brought under exploitation. In this case, expanded reproduction is not homothetic, and relative prices change through the effect of differential rents. When social conditions permit, the appearance of absolute rents (for minerals, for instance) takes place in a setting which accords a role to demand (price "ceilings" dictated by the possibilities of finding substitutes, and so on). Here, too, the problem of how classless society will regulate this question of demand lies outside the scope of this work.

Having said that, we need to go beyond an analysis, in metastatic terms, of successive general equilibria of supply and demand—corresponding to given states of the struggles and alliances between classes—to grasp the dynamic of the dialectic between class struggles and objective economic base, the only way in which we can understand the evolution (transition) from one state to another.

If it is to be carried out effectively, this type of dialectical analysis implies that we take the exact measure of the fundamental contradiction of the capitalist mode. This contradiction counterposes the nature of the productive process, which becomes more and more social as the productive forces develop, to the nature of the production relations, which remain cramped and cramping, being based upon private, fragmented control of the means of production. This analysis thus must be organized around a central axis: the increasingly collective character of the genesis of surplus value, reflecting the ever more markedly social character of production.

This is why, under the capitalist system, the genesis of surplus value cannot be detected without reference to the laws governing its distribution. The genesis of surplus value is already largely collective even at the level of the elementary unit of the system, the capitalist productive enterprise. It appears even more clearly as being collective when we consider the functioning—the reproduction—of a formation, and still more so when we look at the reproduction of the world capitalist system.

At the level of the elementary unit we see manifestations of this collective character, its effects, and the appearances behind which it is hidden. The hierarchical structure of wage levels has no objective basis in productivity or skill: it results from the class struggle and within that struggle, to a large extent, from the strategies pursued by capital not only on the scale of the enterprise but also on that of society. The rationale of this hierarchical structure, concealed by ideology ("differences in productivity of skill," and so on), is governed by class alliances which constitute the means of social reproduction (in particular, the social-democratic and revisionist alliances). We know that, at the level of the elementary unit of capitalist production, surplus value is produced by the "collective laborer." Surplus value is not the sum of the surplus value produced by each of the individual workers: it results from the exploitation by capital of the organized group which constitutes the collective productive worker. In its turn, the value of the collective labor power is shared out among the individuals who compose it in accordance with laws related to the strategies of the class struggle (strategies of capital aimed at splitting the working class, and strategies of labor aimed at strengthening the unity of the exploited). At the same time, the collective surplus value is distributed between capital—the *raison d'être* of which is, precisely, to appropriate this—and certain strata and classes which are allied with capital in the organizing of exploitation (nonproductive wage earners whose jobs result from the fragmentation of the function of organizing the productive process under the rule of capital).

At the level of the formation Marx already suggests the collective character of surplus value in the unpublished sixth chapter of *Capital* ("Results of the Immediate Process of Production"). The price mechanisms, in their broadest sense, here express the way in which it is distributed. This distribution functions at the ideological level (the ideology of economism) no less than at the level of the base. As capitalism develops, the collective character of the genesis of surplus value becomes more marked. The "collective laborer" is less and less definable by observing the organization of the productive process within a single elementary unit. The intensification of productive exchanges between these units; the centralization of capital, which takes away the "commodity" character of these exchanges by internalizing them within the firm; the increasingly composite character of the products of a single firm; the control by financial groups which unify the strategies of capital on the scale of sets of firms integrated both horizontally and vertically, and even of composite groups producing a variety of goods (conglomerates)—all these developments testify to the increasingly social character of the productive process. The field within which the individual workers have their places as constituent elements of the "collective laborer" expands, gradually overflowing the limits of the elementary unit to embrace entire sectors of the economy and even the social formation as a whole. At the same time, distribution of the collective surplus value brings into play struggles and alliances between classes on the scale of the social formation in its entirety.

At the level of the world system, the collective character of the way the surplus product extorted by capitalist exploitation is generated on the world scale is also hidden behind economic appearances which are subjected to ideological treatment. The imperialist hierarchy of rates of exploitation, like the mechanisms whereby the surplus labor generated in the noncapitalist modes is appropriated by dominant capital, are justified by theories of underdevelopment. This ideologizing meets a favorable reception even among Marxists, where it reveals the presence of a pro-imperialist trend based on the social-democratic and revisionist alliance.

My only prupose is to tear off these ideological masks by giving the class struggles their true dimension, which is worldwide. It is therefore necessary to tackle directly the questions of the class struggles on the world scale, of how they are interlinked, and, consequently, of the articulation of modes of production in a system globally dominated by imperialist capital. Here, as I have said, runs the line of fissure between a dogmatic and reactionary interpretation of Marxism that serves to mask the adherence of those who practice it to the pro-imperialist camp, and the revolutionary interpretation.

3. However, before continuing to expound my conclusions regarding the collective genesis of surplus value on the world scale, and before analyzing the reactions to this question on the part of the different trends claiming to be Marxist, it is

important to see clearly how capitalism's fundamental contradiction might be overcome.

I have tried elsewhere to show that for this contradiction there are two possible historical "ways out."[3]

The first is the communist "way out," after a socialist transition period. This is characterized by the establishment of direct correspondence between the social character of the process of production and that of the social relations. It implies not merely the abolition of classes and exploitation but also, of course, the abolition of value, the very existence of which shows that the contradiction has not been overcome. This correspondence therefore puts an end to the economy as an independent sphere, and establishes the direct dominance, without any economic mediation, of society's control over its own future development.

The second is the "way out" constituted by the statist mode of production, which ensures, by the centralization of capital on this scale, that the contradiction is shifted to a higher level of the development of the productive forces. In this case what is presented as the socialist transition is deprived of that character, becoming a new mode of exploitation, which is stable—though no more eternal than capitalism will have been. This is why the Trotskyist theory of the "degenerated workers' state" is without any scientific value. The evolution of economic theory, and a certain convergence between bourgeois theory and Marxian political economy, testify, on the ideological plane, to the historical possibility of this second "way out."

Bourgeois vulgar economic theory corresponded to the state of a capitalist system apparently governed by spontaneous economic laws resulting from behavior by individual firms which was "rational" (at the microeconomic level). Basically, this theory did not concern itself with the macro-economic functioning of the system, except with respect to regulation of the trade cycle by state intervention in the monetary sphere and in that of external competition. Essentially, this theory was therefore an ideological justification of the alleged "universal harmonies" ensuring convergence between individual rationality and interest, on the one hand, and collective rationality and interest, on the other. A theory of this sort did not aim to be an effective instrument for action, but merely an element in the so-called cultural education of the citizenry, meaning their subjection to bourgeois ideology.

The actual evolution of the system, by bringing its basic contradiction more strongly to the forefront; the challenging of capitalism by the Russian and Chinese revolutions; the crisis of the 1930s and the intensification of working class struggles which accompanied this; the rise of the national liberation movements—all led gradually, first, to Keynes's disjointed theorizings, and then, with Sraffa, to a radical return to empiricist macroeconomic analysis, rooted in Ricardo. Economic theory formulated in these terms changes its function, claiming to become an effective instrument of macroeconomic action; but it conceals the interventions which it inspires behind the smokescreen of the alleged economic laws framing the class struggle. This theory therefore corresponds perfectly to the requirements of the macroeconomic management of monopoly capital. The latter, in its turn, can operate effectively only under the favorable political conditions ensured by the hegemony of social democracy in the working class. It therefore has for its foundation the permanence of the imperialist order, relegating the most glaring contradictions to the system's periphery.

Arriving at this point, bourgeois economic theory has drawn considerably closer to the economistic interpretation of Marxism. With the goal of communism forgotten, the emphasis laid on subordination to the "requirements for the development of the productive forces" justifies replacement of the capitalist mode by the statist mode. The gradual transition to state centralization of capital is paralleled by the "growing over" of the old, social-democratic revisionism into the new statist revisionism.

4. We can now appreciate the profound objective connection between the pro-imperialist tendency among Marxists and the social-democratic and statist forms of revisionism.

The objective basis of the pro-imperialist tendency among Marxists is constituted by the fact of imperialism itself and its implication: the hegemony of the social-democratic and revisionist ideologies among the working classes at the center of the system. On the theoretical plane, this tendency finds expression in the tirelessly renewed striving to eliminate the question of the collective, worldwide genesis of surplus value and its distribution. This elimination leads to results which conform in every way to the requirements of the statist "way out." It puts an end to proletarian internationalism, which, in our time, can only mean anti-imperialist solidarity with the peoples of the periphery. Also, it maintains the continued domination of the economistic ideology of commodity relations and value in the working classes of the center. Thereby it justifies the permanence of exploitation, both internal (by renewing the economic arguments about the neutrality of techniques, the division of labor, differences in productivity, and the like) and external (differences of productivity on the world scale). Thus the elimination of the question of collective surplus value on the world scale shows why and how "a people that exploits another people cannot itself be free."

It is interesting to observe that, whatever the school or the line of research, the arguments brought against analyses which are based squarely on class struggle on the world scale are always the same. They include dogmatic assertion of exclusive interest in production relations (reduced, in fact, to relations within the elementary unit of advanced capitalism), which makes it possible to evade, under the pretext of "anti-circulationism," analysis of the collective and worldwide genesis of surplus value. However, theoretical dogmatism often serves as a screen for counterrevolution. One ought to be well aware of this, after the examples given by Kautsky and later by the Soviet Academy. Indeed, these critics forget the ABCs of Marxism: value is not a category of the process of production but of the whole process of production and circulation, since value does not exist without exchange. The dogmatism in question conceals a basic economism: all the arguments directed against analysis of class relations in a system divided into centers and peripheries are ideological justifications for the super-exploitation of the periphery, and are identical with those arguments which justify differences in wage levels within an enterprise by reference to differences of productivity, skill, responsibility, and so on.

The theoretical and practical sterility of the pro-imperialist trend among Marxists has recently been acknowledged by a victim of this trend, Perry Anderson.[4] He categorizes as "Western Marxism" all those trends, which he himself admits to be pessimistic, issued from the defeat of the working-class movement, without impact on reality, and without revolutionary praxis. But, curiously enough, he forgets to explain the reasons for the social-democratic hegemony in the working classes of the advanced centers and does not concern himself with imperialism. He is obliged to discuss at length philosophers whose importance I doubt to be as great as Western opinion would like to believe, and some whom I think can hardly be considered Marxists. On the other hand, when this author comes to mention the trends of "non-Western" Marxism, he goes on about Trotskyism, yet utterly forgets China and Maoism. Not often has anyone mistaken to this extent his personal sympathies and antipathies for major objective realities. I counterpose to this a conception of today's Marxism which starts from recognition of reality—the shift to the periphery of the real forces which profess Marxism—if only so that account may be taken of this fact, even though this means noting some of its negative consequences. For Marxism cannot develop without reference to important struggles, those which transform history.

It is interesting to observe that Perry Anderson's naive admission sets "Western Marxism" exclusively in the field of theory—one might even, without exaggerating, say the academic field—and makes no reference to actual struggles. And this is not accidental. The practical sterility of this "Marxism" is even more glaring than its theoretical sterility. (Anderson tries to contrast an alleged theoretical richness to the practical sterility. He forgets that the purpose of Marxism is not to interpret the world but to change it.)[5]

What are the reasons for this practical sterility? Can one overlook, in this connection, the hegemony of social-democratic revisionism, or the hegemony divided between the revisionisms of the social democrats and the communist parties? And what do attempts at revolution stumble over? For a revolutionary trend does exist, even though it is in the minority, and it finds expression all across southern Europe. Is not the blocking of this trend, for the moment at least—in Portugal or Italy, for instance, not to speak of France or Great Britain—entirely due to this incapacity to think about society otherwise than as part of the imperialist system?[6] It is not only the demands of the Atlantic alliance that are involved, but also the everyday economic reality of Atlantic and European integration and the interests of the imperialist monopolies which have enmeshed the peoples of the West, imposing upon them a solidarity "against the Third World" of which commonplace racism is far from being the only manifestation: the fanatical hostility to China shown by the anarchists and the Trotskyists, the "theory" of the Asiatic mode of production, and all the denunciations of the Third World, even if expressed in leftist terms, are also part of it.

But the trends which understand this—Otelo in Portugal, for instance—still remain, even in southern Europe, minority trends. Trotskyism hopes to answer the question by a verbal "flight forward" which exempts from action: "the revolution will be worldwide." Meanwhile, the revolution is not worldwide, and under these conditions it must be recognized that the driving force of history has been, since the end of the last century and up to our own day, that class struggle which, in the periphery of the system, has for its setting the anti-imperialist fight for national liberation.

By rejecting the preeminence of the fact of imperialism and of its effects on the class struggles on the world scale, by refusing to see national liberation as forming part of the crisis of capitalism and the transition to socialism, and not of the development of capitalism, "Western" Marxism gives naive expression to its pro-imperialist bias.

The fact of imperialism has certainly not suppressed the class struggle at the center. On the contrary, it has intensified the economic dimension of this struggle, but at the expense of its political outlook. The organization of the working class under the social-democratic hegemony integrates the workers in the bourgeois nation, whether one likes this or not, and makes them stand shoulder to shoulder with their bourgeoisie in relation to external competition. Under these conditions, internal economic victories activate international struggles.[7]

In practice, we encounter this expression daily in the predominant "progams of government" of the labor movement, both social-democratic and revisionist. This observation, however decisive it may be, is so undeniable that no revolutionary can doubt it. In the domain of theory, however, since what we are dealing with is a "theoretical" Marxism, examples of the expression of the pro-imperialist trend are no less frequent. Here is a selection.

First example: the return to the bourgeois theory of stages of development in place of the Leninist thesis of imperialism and uneven development. An excellent example is provided by the British Trotskyist Geoffrey Kay, who "shows" that the underdeveloped countries are underdeveloped not because they are super-exploited by capital, but because they are not exploited enough. Such "Marxism," which I have called "Marxism à la Cecil Rhodes" is compatible, for this writer, with a pro-Zionist attitude.[8]

Second example: substitution of the political economy of the multinational corporations for historical materialism. This typically economistic manner of analyzing capitalism is not only preponderant among American radicals (who form an ideological trend engaging in a petty-bourgeois critique of the "misdeeds" of the monopolies), but makes its way into "Western" Marxism through the channel of studies concerning the "world productive process." Embarking on a formal analysis of this process on the basis of observation of the firms involved, without inserting this analysis in the much more fundamental analysis of the class struggle on the world scale, will not enable us to answer the real question of our time: What is the outcome of the struggle? Palloix provides a sad example of the gradual sterilization of this "Marxism." Having dared, in his first book, to tackle the question of the international division of labor in relation to the international class alliances, he quickly abandoned this fruitful line of thought to embark upon a series of formal dissections of the productive process, the increasing obscurity of which witnesses to their sterility.[9]

The trend concerned with the "economy of the multinationals" reveals its helplessness when it is a question of analyzing the present crisis. This trend refuses to see the crisis for what it is: a crisis in the international and national class alliances resulting from changes in the class struggle on the world scale—that is, above all, a crisis of imperialism, having as its immediate expression a crisis of the international division of labor. Having rejected this line of thought, the writers here referred to seek the causes of the crisis inside the central economies, especially that of the United States, and in doing so fail to offer us anything more than we get from the innumerable bourgeois analysts of the phenomenon.[10]

Third example: the philosophers who devote themselves to Marxian exegetics. and who make up the bulk of the Trotskyist cohort and of the revisionist and semirevisionist academicians. With the writers of this trend analysis of imperialism is a mere epiphenomenon. See, for instance, the account of imperialism given by Valier, who forgets the political aspect of the matter (the social-democratic hegemony), retaining only its technical aspect (the monopolies).[11] The *ouvriérisme* characteristic of this trend is always accompanied by stern condemnation of struggles for national liberation, which—being "peasant" and "bourgeois" in character—are of no interest.

Fourth example: ethnography, which connects the modes of production based on class exploitation with a so-called domestic mode of production, transhistorical in character, the focus of the "eternal" exploitation of women by men. Marshall Sahlins and others who have followed him have tried in this way to substitute the domestic mode for analysis of the precapitalist peasant modes of production, thereby erasing the *modus operandi* of the specific exploitation which imperialism imposes on the dominated peasants of the periphery.[12] To this sideslipping I counterpose the analysis made by Rey,[13] which shows how, behind each super-exploited proletarian in the periphery, there are ten peasants who are no less exploited (and for the benefit of the same imperialist capital and its subordinate allies). This exploitation is expressed in the provision of the agricultural surplus needed to reproduce the labor power of the proletarian in question under conditions in which the goods produced (within settings that are formally noncapitalist) are always sold below their value. Rey arrived at this result by analyzing the way subjected peasant modes function, without calling to his aid any transhistorical domestic mode of production *à la* Sahlins. Here we have a theoretical basis for the revolutionary worker–peasant alliance which illustrates the fact that Marxism is always revolutionary.

Fifth example: the historiography of the "European miracle" and the peremptory assertion that all the precapitalist non-European societies were doomed to indefinite stagnation. Tökei and his pupils (in France, for example, Godelier) have in this way turned the "Asiatic mode of production" into a weapon of anti-Maoist polemic with somewhat racist overtones.[14] Subsequently, this thesis has proved to be the Trojan horse by means of which the "new philosophers" of "antitotalitarianism" have smuggled in Weberian idealism, or even, more prosaically, "publicity philosophy" in the service of the policy of the bourgeoisie.[15]

5. The dialectical relation between class struggle and economic base, which constitutes the very essence of historical materialism, is thus without meaning unless we place each of its terms in its true setting; the world capitalist system. This is actually where the frontier runs between pre-Leninist Marxism and Marxism-Leninism-Maoism.

Leninism is not one school of "theoretical" Marxism among others, but the expression of the revolutionary trend in the imperialist epoch. Practice has therefore led it to take up positions in all spheres of social life. Hence the richness of its expression, its many facets: Lenin analyzes imperialism, advocates forms of party organization, organizes in a practical way the revolutionary onslaught, defines the economic policy of the worker–peasant alliance, explains the role of the institutions of the dictatorship of the proletariat, takes a stand in philosophy, and so on. This richness also has its historical limitations: like the Marxism of Marx, Leninism is not to be understood as a finished dogma, a revealed religion.

The lines that separate it from social-democratic deterioration emerged gradually from practical struggle, and therefore retain, if we know how to place them historically, their own ambiguities and imperfections. For example, it seems to me that Leninism retains traces of the mechanical-materialist reduction which was manifested in the "naturalist" outlook of Kautskyism (forerunner of "Diamat"): hence Lenin's "astonishment" when Kautsky joined the social-chauvinist camp.

The richness of Leninism allows for the possibility of understanding Lenin in a variety of ways. It is interesting that in the West the debate about Leninism is concerned almost exclusively with the Lenin of *What Is to Be Done?*—that is, with the question of the organization of the working class and its vanguard.[16] Lenin's *Imperialism* is, however, not much discussed: approved of unanimously, without argument, it is also stripped of its significance.

I see Leninism in quite a different light. The central work is, in my view, *Imperialism*, because it defines the new conditions of the class struggle on the world scale. Here the vital points are made that the historical phase of bourgeois revolutions is finished ("Imperialism, the *highest* stage of capitalism"); that the epoch of socialist revolution is opening; that the social-democratic hegemony at the center has as its objective basis imperialist exploitation; that the national liberation movement is henceforth an integral part of the rising world socialist revolution, and no longer part of the bourgeois revolution. On this basis Lenin defines the strategy of the revolution on the world scale as beginning with the weak links of the system, meaning the peripheries where the revolutionary proletariat can draw in its wake the exploited peasantry who, at the center, are historically the reserves of the bourgeoisie. Thus, Lenin lays down the strategy of *the uninterrupted revolution by stages*, based on the hegemony of the proletariat in the bourgeois stage of the revolution.

The problems of organization must, in my view, be looked at in this setting, for they are always derivative, not primary. Lenin thinks about organization in connection with these new conditions which make the periphery the weak link. In the periphery bourgeois democracy does not exist (it exists at the center only thanks to triumphant imperialism and the rallying thereto of the working class); the proletariat is a minority; it can and must draw into the struggle broad peasant masses which cannot be organized like the working class; the intelligentsia, which at the center is in the service of capital, is here, in the periphery, in the camp of revolution, and so on.

Leninism is meaningless if one does not understand it as the Marxism of the imperialist epoch, and imperialism not merely as "monopoly capitalism" but as monopoly capitalism extracting an increasing proportion of surplus labor from the exploitation of the peoples of the periphery. The reproduction of the social-democratic order at the center thus implies the development of a revolutionary situation in the periphery.

This thesis of Lenin's can doubtless be discussed and even rejected. This was done by the social democrats, who refused to admit that the era of upward capitalist development was over (because, being West-centered, they were indifferent to the rest of the world and made themselves open accomplices of imperialist exploitation). But a number of Western revolutionaries also did this. Some of them, perhaps, had not been able to break away sufficiently from their West-centered background. Others had presentiments of certain shortcomings of the Russian revolution. Hence some "dialogues of the deaf," explicit or implicit, between Lenin, on the one hand, and, on the other, Rosa Luxemburg, Gramsci, Pannekoek, Adler, and the "Workers'-Councils-Communists" known as the "Lefts," and so on. The subsequent evolution of Soviet Russia was to reactivate the critique of Leninism. It is interesting to note that this contemporary critique comes, in the West, usually from the Right: it revives the ideas of social democracy and even assumes, in its extreme caricatured form, the aspect we see presented by the proponents of the "new philosophy." Trotskyism, which claims to be Leninist, is not so at all: its rigorously West-centered outlook contradicts that of Leninism and compels it to remain bogged down in dogmatic exegesis. As for the trends of that famous "Western Marxism" mentioned above, they are all linked with trends in bourgeois, and therefore pre-Marxist, philosophy. Consequently, even when they ask the right questions, they are incapable of answering these questions because their society is not ready for the answers. Refusing to break with imperialism, they can be and are reabsorbed, especially through psychologism in one form or another (Freudo-Marxism, feminism, and so on).

On the other side, the critique of Leninism from the Left—that is, the solving in practice of the problems presented by Leninism constitutes the contribution made by Maoism. The limitations and ambiguities of Leninism are not situated "upstream"—in its analysis of imperialism and its way of deducing the consequences in respect of strategy and organization—but "downstream," in its inadequate answers to the problems of the worker–peasant dictatorship. The practice and the theory of the class struggle in the phase of the socialist transition, as this has presented itself in reality, have been developed by Maoism on the basis of Leninism—that is, on the basis of the fundamental achievements of Leninism, within the framework of a Marxism which remains the Marxism of the imperialist epoch and its crisis. What the inadequacies of this remarkable step forward may prove to be, what problems it will present to the generations to come, are for history to reveal. Future struggles alone will produce the answers.

NOTES

INTRODUCTION

1. Carlo Benetti, *Valeur et répartition* (Paris: Maspero, 1975); C. Benetti, C. Berthomieu, and J. Cartelier, *Economie classique, économie vulgaire* (Paris: Maspero, 1975).
2. When M. Dowidar, in *L'économie politique, une science sociale* (Paris: Maspero, 1974), describes political economy as "the science of the modes of production," he is confusing, it seems to me, political economy with historical materialism.
3. Paper presented at a colloquium on precapitalist societies organized at the University of Vincennes in 1977 and published in Samir Amin and Andre Gunder Frank, *Accumulation, dépendance, et sous-développement* (Paris: Anthropos, 1977).
4. Ibid.

1. THE FUNDAMENTAL STATUS OF THE LAW OF VALUE

1. Samir Amin, "The End of the Debate," in *Imperialism and Unequal Development* (New York: Monthly Review Press, 1977), p. 242.
2. Benetti, for instance, in *Valeur et répartition* (Paris, Maspero,

1975). This is also A. Emmanuel's view in his *Unequal Exchange* (New York: Monthly Review Press, 1972), pp. 390 ff.

3. In *Labor and Monopoly Capital* (New York: Monthly Review Press, 1974).

4. There is a summary of this ill-formulated debate in Amin, "The End of the Debate," in *Imperialism and Unequal Development*, pp. 223–25. See also Amin, *Unequal Development* (New York: Monthly Review Press, 1976), pp. 59–63.

5. Ibid., pp. 45–46.

6. See my criticism of this idea in *Unequal Development*, pp. 226–29, which is repeated by Jean Cartelier in *Surproduit et répartition* (Paris: Maspero, 1976), pp. 200–02.

7. *Unequal Development*, pp. 24–26.

8. My criticism of neoclassical economics and its circular reasoning about the productivity of the factors goes back to 1957. The same criticism, applied to the "assumption of the unit of account [*postulat du numéraire*]," is to be found in Jacques Fradin, *Les fondements logiques de la théorie néo-classique de l'échange* (Paris: Maspero, 1976).

9. A remarkable demonstration of the dead-end character of neoclassical economics is given in Benetti, *Valeur et répartition*.

10. *Unequal Development*, pp. 226 ff.

11. Ibid., pp. 59–72.

2. POLITICAL ECONOMY AND HISTORICAL MATERIALISM

1. Amin, "The End of the Debate," in *Imperialism and Unequal Development* (New York: Monthly Review Press, 1977), pp. 195–208 and Appendix.

2. Ibid., pp. 197–98; *Unequal Development* (New York: Monthly Review Press, 1976), pp. 84–88. The nature of state management of credit will be analyzed in Chapter 3.

3. S. de Brunhoff, *L'offre de monnaie: Etat et capital. Recherches sur la politique économique* (Paris: Maspero, 1976), for example, leaves the reader unsatisfied by failing to show how the demand for money is connected with accumulation.

4. Confusion concerning the dispute between Luxemburg and Lenin about the market question persists among all those who overlook the active role played by money in accumulation (see Palloix, Meillassoux, etc.).
5. These cases are discussed in "The End of the Debate," in *Imperialism and Unequal Development*, pp. 195–205.
6. The best example of this is Michio Morishima, *Marx's Economics* (Cambridge and New York: Cambridge University Press, 1973).
7. "The End of the Debate," in *Imperialism and Unequal Development*, pp. 205–08 and 250–52.
8. Ibid., pp. 206–07.

3. INTEREST, MONEY, AND THE STATE

1. *Imperialism and Unequal Development* (New York: Monthly Review Press, 1977), Chapter 2.
2. *Unequal Development* (New York: Monthly Review Press, 1976), pp. 84–88.
3. See *Unequal Development*, pp. 104–32.
4. On this plane, the analyses of S. de Brunhoff, though they stay too close to mere exegesis of Marx where the supply of money is concerned, have very properly reminded us of the close relation between the state and money which is intrinsic to the analysis given in *Capital*.

4. GROUND RENT

1. Carlo Benetti, *Valeur et répartition* (Paris: Maspero, 1975).
2. Henri Regnault, *La contradiction foncière* (thesis, Paris, 1975; mimeo).
3. *Imperialism and Unequal Development* (New York: Monthly Review Press, 1977), Chapter 2.
4. Claude Berthomieu, *Eléments de réflexion théoriques sur la théorie de la rente en économie politique* (Nice, 1977; mimeo).

5. Alain Lipietz, *Le tribut foncier urbain* (Paris: Maspero, 1974);
P. P. Rey, *Les alliances de classe* (Paris: Maspero, 1973); Gilles
Postel-Vinay, *La rente foncière dans le capitalisme agricole* (Paris:
Maspero, 1974); Claude Faure, *Agriculture et mode de production
capitaliste* (thesis, University of Vincennes, to be published by
Anthropos in 1978); Bruno Lautier, *La soumission formelle du
travail au capital* (Vincennes); Amin, *Imperialism and Unequal
Development*, Chapter 2.
6. See the history of this development as given by Claude Faure.
7. A. Benachenhou, *La formation du sous-développement de l'Algerie,
1830-1960* (Algiers, 1976).

5. THE IMPERIALIST SYSTEM

1. See *Imperialism and Unequal Development* (New York: Monthly
Review Press, 1977), Introduction and chapters 5 and 6.
2. Ibid., pp. 34–43.
3. *Unequal Development* (New York: Monthly Review Press, 1976),
pp. 104–32.
4. Published in *Tiers Monde*, no. 52 (1972), and reproduced in *Unequal Development*, pp. 72–78 and 191–97.
5. *Unequal Development*, pp. 131–32.

6. THE THEORY AND PRACTICE OF MINING RENT

1. An observation made, among others, by Amilcar O. Herrera et al.,
Catastrophe or New Society (I.D.R.C., 1976).
2. *Imperialism and Unequal Development* (New York: Monthly Review
Press, 1977), chapters 1 and 7.
3. Ibid., Chapter 7.
4. Ibid., Chapter 5; and Amin, Faire, Hussein, and Massiah, *La crise de
l'impérialisme* (Paris: Minuit, 1975).
5. "Développement autocentre, autonomie collective et ordre économique international nouveau," in Amin and Frank, *Accumulation,
dépendance, et sous-développement* (Paris: Anthropos, 1977).

6. "The End of the Debate," in *Imperialism and Unequal Development*, p. 210.
7. See J. M. Chevalier, *Le nouvel enjeu petrolier* (Paris, 1973), and *La crise mondiale du capitalisme* (University of Vincennes, 1975).
8. Yvon Le Moal, *L'avenir du contrôle du minerai de fer et ses implications pour les relations sidérurgiques internationales* (Montpellier: G.R.E.S.E., 1976; mimeo).

APPENDIX

1. C. Benetti, C. Berthomieu, and J. Cartelier, *Economie classique, économie vulgaire* (Paris: Maspero, 1975).
2. See above, and also *Imperialism and Unequal Development* (New York: Monthly Review Press, 1977), Chapter 2 (on rent) and "The End of the Debate," pp. 225 ff. (on the tendency of the rate of profit to fall).
3. Appendix to "The End of the Debate" (on the theory of money); *Unequal Development* (New York: Monthly Review Press, 1976), pp. 84 ff. (theory of money) and pp. 92 ff. (theory of the cycle).
4. Appendix to "The End of the Debate," see above reference to *Unequal Development*, pp. 84 ff., and criticism of the inadequacies of the interpretation of Marx on money given by, among others, Suzanne de Brunhoff in *L'offre de monnaie* (Paris: Maspero, 1976).
5. *Unequal Development*, pp. 226 ff. This recalls Marx's criticism of Adam Smith when the latter reduces the value of production to an infinite sum of incomes (wages and profits) engendered over past time.
6. On this point Suzanne de Brunhoff (*L'offre de monnaie*) has reminded us that, for Marx, money is not a "veil," but enters actively into exchange, which takes place not as exchange of commodity for commodity but of commodity for money and money for commodity.
7. *Unequal Development*, p. 84.
8. Benetti, Berthomieu, and Cartelier, *Economie classique, économie vulgaire*, pp. 71 ff.
9. This is argued in *Unequal Development*, pp. 23 ff.

CONCLUSION

1. A. Bodanov, *La science, l'art et la classe ouvrière* (Paris: Maspero, 1977).

2. Amin, *Imperialism and Unequal Development* (New York: Monthly Review Press, 1977), Chapter 4, "Universality and Cultural Spheres."

3. "La bourgeoisie est-elle encore une classe montante?" in Amin and Frank, *Accumulation, dépendance, et sous-développement* (Paris: Anthropos, 1977).

4. Perry Anderson, *Considerations on Western Marxism* (New York: Humanities, 1976).

5. S. Amin, "Le marxisme après 1945," in *Le marxisme* (Paris: Encyclopédie Larousse, 1977).

6. See, on this subject, the excellent analyses concerning Portugal, in CEDETIM, *L'expérience portugaise* (Paris: Maspero, 1977), and Italy, in Yves Benot, *L'autre Italie, 1968–1976* (Paris: Maspero, 1977).

7. See my introduction to Beaud, Bellon, and François, *Lire le capitalisme* (Paris: Anthropos, 1976); see also my contribution in Amin and Frank, *Accumulation, dépendance, et sous-développement.*

8. G. Kay, *Development, Underdevelopment, and the Law of Value: A Marxist Analysis* (New York: St. Martin, 1975). See my criticism in Amin and Frank, *Accumulation, dépendance, et sous-développement*; also in *The Insurgent Sociologist*, issue on "Imperialism and the State," University of Oregon, Spring 1977.

9. Palloix's first book was *Les problèmes de la croissance en économie ouverte* (Paris: Maspero, 1969). I contrast with this his latest writings: *L'internationalisation du capital* (Paris: Maspero, 1975), inspired by the theses made popular by R. Vernon, *Sovereignty at Bay: The Multinational Spread of U.S. Enterprises* (London: Longman, 1971), *Les entreprises multinationales* (Paris, 1973), and *Procès de production et crise du capitalisme* (Paris: Maspero, 1977).

10. For analyses of the crisis made from the standpoint criticized, see Palloix's *Works*; Vladimir Andreff, *Profits et strucutres du capitalisme mondial* (Paris: Calmann-Lévy, 1976); and some analyses

published in *La crise mondiale du capitalisme* (University of Vincennes, 1975). In contrast to this type of analysis one can mention Amin, Faire, Hussein, and Massiah, *La crise de l'impérialisme et le développement inégal* (Paris: Minuit, 1976); see also A. Faire and J. P. Sebord, *Le nouveau déséquilibre mondial* (Paris: Grasset, 1973); *Face à la crise*, in *Cahiers pour le Communisme*, nos. 2 and 3 (1975); A Farhi, Y. Fitt, and J. P. Vigier, *La crise de l'impérialisme et la troisième guerre mondiale* (Paris: Maspero, 1976).

11. See my critique in the introduction to Beaud, Bellon, and François, *Lire le capitalisme*.

12. See my critique of the "concept" of the domestic mode of production introduced by M. Sahlins and taken up by numerous anthropologists (among others, Meillassoux: *Femmes, greniers et capitaux* [Paris: Maspero, 1976]), in Amin and Frank, *Accumulation, dépendance, et sous-développement* ("A quoi sert l'étude des sociétés pré-capitalistes").

13. Besides P. P. Rey's principal writings (published by Maspero), I refer here to his *Transfert de plus-value et articulations des modes de production*, an unpublished duplicated document.

14. See my critique of Tökei in Amin and Frank, *Accumulation, dépendance, et sous-développement*.

15. As has been well said by François Aubral and Xavier Deltrout, *Contre la nouvelle philosophie*, Collection "Idees," 1977. See also Gilles Deleuze, "A propos des nouveaux philosophes et d'un problème plus général," supplement to *Minuit 24*.

16. Here I am referring to the predominant, anarchistic trend among the critics of Leninism. With this I contrast serious analyses of the historical limitations of Leninism such as those made by the *Manifesto* group in Italy (see *Il Manifesto* [Paris: Seuil, 1971]), or by M. Liebman (*Leninism Under Lenin* [London: Jonathan Cape, 1975]), Sigrid Grosskopf (*L'alliance ouvrière et paysanne en URSS, 1921-1928* [Paris: Maspero, 1976]), Carmen Claudín-Urondo (*Lenin and the Cultural Revolution* [Hassocks: Harvester Press, 1977]), Robert Linhart (*Lénine, les paysans, Taylor* [Paris: Seuil, 1976]), or the monumental analysis of Charles Bettelheim (*Class Struggles in the U.S.S.R.* [two volumes published, New York: Monthly Review Press, 1977 and 1978]).